C. S. Lewis

WHO WROTE THAT?

C. S. Lewis

John Davenport

Foreword by
Kyle Zimmer

Chelsea House Publishers
Philadelphia

CHELSEA HOUSE PUBLISHERS

VP, NEW PRODUCT DEVELOPMENT Sally Cheney
DIRECTOR OF PRODUCTION Kim Shinners
CREATIVE MANAGER Takeshi Takahashi
MANUFACTURING MANAGER Diann Grasse

STAFF FOR C. S. LEWIS

ASSOCIATE EDITOR Benjamin Kim
PICTURE RESEARCHER Pat Holl
PRODUCTION ASSISTANT Megan Emery
SERIES DESIGNER Keith Trego
LAYOUT 21st Century Publishing and Communications, Inc.

http://www.chelseahouse.com

First Printing

1 3 5 7 9 8 6 4 2

Library of Congress Cataloging-in-Publication Data applied for.

ISBN 0-7910-7620-2

Table of Contents

FOREWORD BY
KYLE ZIMMER
PRESIDENT, FIRST BOOK

HUMANITY IS POWERED by stories. From our earliest days as thinking beings, we employed every available tool to tell each other stories. We danced, drew pictures on the walls of our caves, spoke, and sang. All of this extraordinary effort was designed to entertain, recount the news of the day, explain natural occurrences—and then gradually to build religious and cultural traditions and establish the common bonds and continuity that eventually formed civilizations. Stories are the most powerful force in the universe; they are the primary element that has distinguished our evolutionary path.

Our love of the story has not diminished with time. Enormous segments of societies are devoted to the art of storytelling. Book sales in the United States alone topped $26 billion last year; movie studios spend fortunes to create and promote stories; and the news industry is more pervasive in its presence than ever before.

There is no mystery to our fascination. Great stories are magic. They can introduce us to new cultures, or remind us of the nobility and failures of our own, inspire us to greatness or scare us to death, but above all, stories provide human insight on a level that is unavailable through any other source. In fact, stories connect each of us to the rest of humanity not just in our own time, but also throughout history.

This special magic of books is the greatest treasure that we can hand down from generation to generation. In fact, that spark in a child that comes from books became the motivation for the creation of my organization, First Book, a national literacy program with a simple mission: to provide new books to the most disadvantaged children. At present, First Book has been at work in hundreds of communities for over a decade. Every year children in need receive millions of books through our organization and millions more are provided through dedicated literacy institutions across the United States and around the world. In addition, groups of people dedicate themselves tirelessly to working with children to share reading and stories in every imaginable setting from schools to the streets. Of course, this Herculean effort serves many important goals. Literacy translates to productivity and employability in life and many other valid and even essential elements. But at the heart of this movement are people who love stories, love to read and want desperately to ensure that no one misses the wonderful possibilities that reading provides.

When thinking about the importance of books, there is an overwhelming urge to cite the literary devotion of great minds. Some have written of the magnitude of the importance of literature. Amy Lowell, an American poet, captured the concept with her statement when she said, "Books are more than books. They are the life, the very heart and core of ages past, the reason why men lived and worked and died, the essence and quintessence of their lives." Others have spoken of their personal obsession with books, as in Thomas Jefferson's simple statement: "I live for books." But more compelling, perhaps, is the almost instinctive excitement in children for books and stories.

Throughout my years at First Book, I have heard truly extraordinary stories about the power of books in the lives of children. In one case, a homeless child, who had been bounced from one location to another, later resurfaced—and the only possession that he had fought to keep was the book he was given as part of a First Book distribution months earlier. More recently, I met a child who, upon receiving the book he wanted, flashed a big smile and said, "This is my big chance!" These snapshots reveal the true power of books and stories to give hope and change lives.

As these children grow up and continue to develop their love of reading, they will owe a profound debt to those volunteers who reached out to them—a debt that they may repay by reaching out to spark the next generation of readers. But there is a greater debt owed by all of us—a debt to the storytellers, the authors, who have bound us together, inspired our leaders, fueled our civilizations, and helped us put our children to sleep with their heads full of images and ideas.

WHO WROTE THAT? is a series of books dedicated to introducing us to a few of these incredible individuals. While we have almost always honored stories, we have not uniformly honored storytellers. In fact, some of the most important authors have toiled in complete obscurity throughout their lives or have been openly persecuted for the uncomfortable truths that they have laid before us. When confronted with the magnitude of their written work or perhaps the daily grind of our own, we can forget that writers are people. They struggle through the same daily indignities and dental appointments, and they experience the intense joy and bottomless despair that many of us do. Yet somehow they rise above it all to deliver a powerful thread that connects us all. It is a rare honor to have the opportunity that these books provide to share the lives of these extraordinary people. Enjoy.

C. S. Lewis (left), shown here with classmate and fellow soldier Paddy Moore. Lewis' stint as a soldier in World War I ended with a friendly-fire shelling accident that left him in a hosptial with shrapnel still lodged in his body.

1

France, 1918

THE HUNGRY, FRIGHTENED young men peered out at a blasted landscape. What they saw resembled a graveyard more than farm fields: frozen, barren ground studded with twisted metal monuments to the destructive power of modern warfare. The driving snow stung their faces while the wind seemed to bring together the cries of thousands of wounded men in its unnerving howl. The armies that faced each other that cold April day had endured nearly three years of stalemate. During that time, both sides longed for a return to the war of movement that had preceded the dull terror of trench warfare. The Germans finally decided in the spring of 1918 to mount a massive offensive that was intended to break open the Western Front in Europe and bring them total victory once and for all.

This tiny sliver of shell-pocked, frozen mud near the French town of Arras sat at the center of their grand scheme. The common infantrymen knew little about strategies and master plans for victory, however, and they cared even less. All they knew was that the contest for this godforsaken place might well kill them all. Huddled together for warmth and solace, the soldiers of the Somerset Light Infantry anxiously waited for the German divisions to slam into their part of the line. Even if they held their positions, the battle would still be far from over. Successful defensive efforts always meant counterattack.

Soon it would be the Somerset Light Infantry's turn to charge into a deadly blizzard of bullets and shrapnel, trying to gain ground that no sane person would desire. Then again, insanity was the rule here. Soon would come the inevitable piercing wail of the commander's whistle ordering them into the assault— "going over the top" as they put it during the First World War.

Suddenly from behind the soldiers, the distant and hollow pop of the big field guns began its slow rise to a terrifying crescendo. No sooner had the dull booming reached their ears than they perceived an even more ominous noise of war—the raspy screeching of outgoing artillery shells passing overhead. Yet instead of the usual faraway thud of impact, the boys gasped as some of the rounds exploded with a crash just in front of their position.

Before that bleak April day, British artillery had commonly torn into the German trenches hundreds, if not thousands, of yards away. The point had been to soften up the German lines prior to the desperate charge of the infantry across the vast expanse of "no-man's-land," the deadly tract of unoccupied ground between the opposing trenches. Now, the shells shook the earth and sent up columns of dirt and rock right in front of the nervous soldiers. The German advance had brought them very close to the British lines—too close it seemed. The artillery had tried to pound the enemy but dropped their shells just forward of their own line.

Eventually, spotters would adjust the firing and walk the rounds slowly into the enemy positions, but for now the British soldiers could only wait and hope that a stray shell let loose by their own troops did not fall amongst them. Each time one of the big guns fired, the men sat helplessly, putting their trust in the accuracy of the British crews. Thus the troops of the Somerset found themselves in double jeopardy, as the threat of German guns only barely surpassed the danger posed by their own supporting fire.

As the shells began to descend from the sky like some murderous hailstorm, Jack sat fearfully among the Light Infantry. Only nineteen years old but already a second lieutenant in the British army, Jack was a typical young officer in this senseless war. Sent to fight at a tender age, he was now a veteran of five months of combat service. Sitting comfortably at a boarding school when the fighting broke out, Jack could never conceive of killing other men. His life had been spent quietly—reading, studying, and, most to his liking, dreaming up stories about imaginary lands. Jack's earliest memories were of hiding away in the attic of the family home with his brother, Warren, inventing worlds that existed only in their own heads. Jack drew on imagery distilled from his father's books and hours spent listening to discussions of politics and religion to create entire make-believe kingdoms.

His fantasy life had been rich indeed, but now he sat cold and wet in the belly of the darkest of realities. Each explosion and whining bullet reminded him of how far he had wandered from the comfort of his attic hideaway. He had seen many men die during his time in France; now he braced himself in anticipation of seeing countless more lives snuffed out. Waiting with the rest of his unit, Jack must have wondered whether the field before him would become his grave as well.

Did you know...

Lewis tested his father's patience sorely while in France. At one point, Albert tried to have his son moved to an artillery regiment. The transfer—to a safer location farther to the rear—would have gone through were it not for resistance from an unexpected source. Lieutenant Lewis himself refused the offer, saying, "I must confess that I have become very attached to this regiment. I have several friends whom I should be sorry to leave and I am just beginning to know my men and understand the work." Soon after writing these words, Lewis was wounded in action.

The contest for this wasteland that the generals and politicians called a battlefield had already raged for almost a month before Jack received news that his end of the line was close to being secured. Over 160,000 British soldiers had been killed or wounded since the beginning of the German spring offensive. As with most men who met their end or shed their blood fighting in World War I, they fell in front of withering machine gun fire, under a pulverizing rain of artillery shells, or choking on the poison gas used so often by both sides. Many of the bodies from the previous weeks' fighting lay exposed on the battlefield, mangled and battered beyond recognition. These young men of Great Britain had surrendered their lives for a few yards of bloody soil that, sooner or later, Jack knew he might have to either cross himself, or at least defend against advancing Germans.

If he had not rejected a belief in any god years before, Jack probably would have prayed for deliverance—but he never had found much relief in religion. His family tree, to be sure, had produced more than its share of clergymen, and Jack's father worshipped and drove his sons to worship in traditional Protestant ways. This meant prayer and study in an effort to discern the hand of God working its will among humans. Jack, however, no matter how hard he tried, never saw that hand. Nor did he grow up to fear God's power and majesty.

Jack had lost his faith long before the war. He was unable to find the comfort, insight, and revelation that he searched for in established Christianity. The young soldier experienced his father's faith as an empty vessel into which lonely people poured their hopes. Jack had hope as well—and so many questions. Christianity, however, remained devoid of answers and left his hopes unfulfilled. The Christian God, Jack felt at this point in his life, was as hard and cold as the stark ground in front of him. So he sat alone in his thoughts near the end of what turned out to be the final days of the German effort to win the war.

Jack most likely never heard the approach of the artillery shell fired by his own side that fell short of its mark and almost on top of him—but its detonation would have deafened him. Men wounded by artillery fire usually recall a blinding flash. Next comes the roar of the explosion, loud enough to blow out a soldier's eardrums. Only then does a man feel the numbing concussion of the shockwave. Picking himself up in a daze, the soldier perceives slowly—but with increasing terror—the searing pain of the hot, jagged metal that just seconds before had ripped into his flesh. Then, men say, seemingly in an instant, the black calm of unconsciousness overcomes them, temporarily relieving their agony. The lucky ones, like Jack, woke up from this nightmare in a hospital bed.

Jack's bed was in the field hospital at Etaples, fifty miles from Arras. Warren, who came to visit Jack, wrote that he was "in great form, expecting to be sent home." As far as the fighting went, Jack was "out of it for a bit." Growing up, his brother Warren had been Jack's closest friend. They read together, took long bicycle rides together in the country, and stoked the fires of each other's imaginations. When formal schooling put the boys in different parts of England and far from their Irish home, Jack longed for reunion. Later in life, Warren and

Brothers Jack (left) and Warren (right) were inseparable companions and shared a deep friendship that would last all their lives. Only geography could separate them, but as soon as Jack's war duties were fulfilled, the two brothers would reunite again.

Jack would be inseparable. Through the ups and downs of Jack's career and through the nightmare of Warren's alcoholism, they would remain friends as well as brothers. The war seemed to be the only thing that could force them apart.

Now here they were, together again in a hospital packed with wounded soldiers. Warren felt confident that Jack would be fine, but the shell had done more damage than he realized. The metal splinters had torn through the back of Jack's hand, and his left leg had been ripped open near the knee. Worst of all, a piece of shrapnel had pierced Jack's chest and was lodged dangerously close to his heart. The doctors decided against removing the metal fragment, because to do so might cost the young lieutenant his life. They thought it better to leave it where it was and hope for the best. Perhaps it might kill him, they figured, but it would be no great loss to the world if one more forlorn soldier, among millions, died on the Western Front.

What went through Jack's mind as he struggled to survive we will never know. Maybe he thought of his beloved mother, taken by cancer some years earlier, or his taciturn father, whom Jack and Warren referred to "Pudaita," mocking the old man's Irish accent whenever he spoke about potatoes. Perhaps he pondered the existence of the Christian God he had rejected as a boy but would come to embrace as a man. Would he ever be able to accept the notion of an all-loving God after what he had witnessed on the battlefields of France?

The answer seemed centuries away as Jack lay in his bed recovering. He might have wondered whether or not he would ever complete the university studies he left to go to war, or write all the stories he dreamed up as a boy, especially the stories about a magical world where good and evil contended relentlessly. The young officer might have contemplated any number of future possibilities and eventualities. Chances are good, however, that Jack had no idea, lying there in the Liverpool Merchants' Mobile

Hospital, how many lives he would touch and how many minds he would reach and stretch—not as Second Lieutenant Jack Lewis, but as the man we know today as the author C. S. Lewis.

C. S. Lewis was born into a loveless home that was luckily offset with a story-telling nanny and a large library of books. A precocious youth, Lewis even came up with a new name that he wished to replace his real first name — "Jack," a name that would be used for the rest of his life.

2

The Little End Room

FLORA AND ALBERT Lewis' second child entered the world rather quietly on November 29, 1898. The Lewises greeted his birth with a degree of reserve typical for the couple. They simply refused to let the new arrival disturb the daily routine of the tidy home outside Belfast, northern Ireland. Whether or not the baby was a cause for joy we will never know. To be sure, the newborn's older brother certainly resented the competition for his parents' limited attention. Flora and Albert's oldest son, Warren, born three years earlier, did not relish the changes his new brother would bring. Warren later described the baby as little more than "a vociferous disturber of my peace." Nevertheless, here he was, a tiny baby boy—Clive.

Little Clive's parents shared an odd ambivalence toward their two sons, marked by alternating urges to embrace and reject the boys. Emotional expression confounded both Albert and Flora; neither seemed able to make sense of their feelings, a trait they passed on to Lewis which he found very troubling in himself. No doubt part of the couple's problem lay in the odd circumstances of a courtship and marriage that brought together a man and a woman for whom love did not come easily. They had to consciously craft the kind of union most young couples take for granted.

When Albert and Flora first met, they could not have been more different. Albert, a man of strict and consistent morals derived from a strong Protestant family heritage, tended to be predictable in his personal life and in his dealings with others. Yet he could be obsessive about routine, and at times he had a tendency to fixate on minor problems. Albert possessed an agile mind, a quick wit, and a powerful imagination, but all of these were overridden by a consuming impulse to order and control everything. There can be no doubt that he worked hard, but his energy was often misspent; Albert had trouble differentiating between the important and the trivial and often struggled through life more than he had to. Still, Albert did become fairly successful, studying law and eventually establishing his own practice.

Flora came from a snobbish, dismissive family of devout Anglicans. Unlike Albert, her background was anything but common. She could—and did for anyone who asked—trace her family line all the way back to the medieval Anglo-Irish nobility. Whereas Albert was the son of a moderately successful and rather nondescript businessman, Flora's father was a fiery and controversial preacher. As the pastor of St. Mark's Church, he made a name for himself by spitting out rabidly anti-Catholic sermons during which he became so agitated that he cried. Such outbursts and excesses embarrassed Flora to no end. They frightened her as well, and led her to craft a personality that emphasized cool reserve, emotional distance, and, above all, predictability.

Albert and Flora thus brought very different qualities into a relationship that began almost by accident, followed by a marriage that took place by default. Flora met Albert through his brother, a man who had courted the minister's daughter intensely before she rejected him as dull and uninspiring. Looking for someone a bit more exciting, Flora turned to Albert. Yet no matter how hard she tried, she could not develop an attraction to him beyond simple friendship. Albert, on the other hand, eagerly pursued Flora, unaware that she felt nothing romantic toward him. The sort of warmth and abandon needed for such emotions eluded her—Flora simply could not reciprocate Albert's feelings, and went so far as to tell him so on one occasion. In an effort to get Albert to stop writing passionate letters to her, Flora coolly informed him that no matter what he offered her, she had nothing "but friendship to give in exchange."

Flora's protestations, however, did not deter Albert; he continued to press her. Their courtship dragged on for seven long years before Albert, now losing interest, came close to ending it. Flora, faced with perhaps spending her life alone, at last rewarded Albert's effort and accepted his proposal of marriage. By then, however, the damage had been done— Albert's emotions had cooled. Their union would be, at best, cordial and businesslike. A certain bond would develop between them, but nothing that resembled the type of love one expects in a marriage. This became clear as early as their honeymoon. Instead of using the time to focus his energy on his new wife, Albert ended the honeymoon early to attend to an important client of his law firm. Flora did not object.

The degree of Flora's detachment from matters of the heart became clear not long after the infant Lewis' birth. Within one month, Flora hired a nurse, Lizzie Endicott, and gave her physical and emotional responsibility for her son. Like his parents, the baby's surrogate mother came out of a staunch Protestant tradition. Unlike them, however, Lizzie brought to her relationship with Lewis a certain warmth and openness that he never forgot. The author recalled how as a child he could "discover no flaw" in Lizzie, "nothing but kindness, gaiety, and good sense." Lizzie more than admirably filled in for Flora. She comforted Lewis and fed his already powerful imagination. Lizzie read to the boy every day and told stories that flowed almost magically out of her proud Irish oral tradition.

Lewis remembered vividly how Lizzie told stories about leprechauns and forest witches through folktales and myths. From them, he drew both joy and inspiration. By comparison, Flora's sole contribution to his early creative development was limited to the unconscionably careless mistake of leaving a peculiar book in Clive's nursery—a picture book portraying a giant beetle attacking a small boy. The resulting nightmares plagued Lewis for the rest of his life and left him with a phobic aversion to insects even as an adult.

Lizzie Endicott nurtured Lewis' imagination, but she also reinforced the already significant role of religion in his world. Her own pervasive beliefs inflamed Lewis' passion for a connection with the divine. He wanted, above all else, a framework upon which he could structure his life and bring order to his creative powers. God and religion offered such a scaffold, but Lewis needed help in adapting his daily existence to something that seemed so vast and incomprehensible to his immature mind. In a less positive sense, Lizzie's anti-Catholic leanings bolstered a growing awareness within him that organized Christianity had a dark side.

Lizzie insisted on referring to Catholics as "filth" and went so far as to refer to mud puddles as "wee popes"—as she thought popes were in charge of a dirty religion. On the one hand, Lizzie conveyed a religious message that emphasized warmth and security; on the other, her condemnation of Catholics and the dark vocabulary of sin that laced her conversations repelled Lewis and planted the seeds of future doubts about God in particular and religion in general.

The extent to which Lizzie imparted an independent streak to her young charge is unknown. She did encourage him to be bold and might have been the inspiration for his proud announcement, at the advanced age of four, that he had decided to rename himself. From that moment on, he would answer to the name Jacksie, which he later shortened to Jacks, and finally to Jack, the nickname he retained into adulthood. The little boy gave no reason for the sudden alteration in his identity, and no one seems to have pressed the matter much. Albert, Flora, and Warren readily acquiesced in the change and humored this early eccentricity. Chances are

Did you know...

While at Little Lea, Lewis and his brother began referring to their father as "Pudaita." Sometimes they called him "pudaitabird," or just "P." The boys also came up with humorous nicknames for each other: together they were the "pigiebothams"— Warren was "Archpigiebotham" or "APB," while Lewis went by the name "Smallpigiebotham" or "SPB." The names were apparently derived from Lizzie Endicott's repeated threats to spank the young pair's "piggie bottoms."

good that this exercise in self-labeling represented the first stirrings of the independence and singular ambition for which the adult Lewis would be well known.

In April 1905, Albert moved the family into a new house which he christened Little Lea. Although Albert was proud of the home for which he had spent a considerable sum, Lewis remembered it as being poorly built and believed that his father had acted foolishly in purchasing it. "My father was badly cheated," Lewis claimed. Warren concurred, remembering Little Lea as "the worst designed house I ever saw," but quickly added that it was "for that very reason a child's delight." The layout and construction of Little Lea left huge open spaces throughout the structure, areas the boys were free to explore and set aside as their own.

The significance of this liberty grew as Albert's surveillance of the boys increased and as the elder Lewis developed a penchant for meddling in his sons' affairs. The dusty nooks and crannies the boys laid claim to became a key element in a complex of ideas and images that fired Lewis' imagination. The author, as an adult, described himself as being "a product of long corridors, empty sunlit rooms, upstairs indoor silences, attics explored in solitude . . ." In such places he could wonder and speculate, free from the constraints imposed by the world his parents occupied in other less secluded parts of the house.

Little Lea, in addition to being a maze of private spaces, was also a veritable library. The house nearly groaned under the weight of Albert and Flora's collection of books. If the two parents shared little else in common, they both had an abiding love of books. Throughout the house, wherever Lewis wandered, books stood ready for the reading. As a child, he "had always the same certainty of finding a book that was new to me as a man who walks into a field has of

The Lewis home at Little Lea, while not the most sturdily constructed home, provided Jack and Warren with endless hours of fun due in part to its odd architecture and their parents' book collection. Their fertile imaginations ran free, especially in a nook they called the Little End Room.

finding a new blade of grass." Yet the family collection was in a way rather limited. Volumes dealing with history, philosophy, and biography could be found easily, but works of poetry or mythology were few if present at all. Lewis could read about politics or great kingdoms whenever he chose, but his appetite for fantasy remained unsatisfied. Little of what he read from his parents' shelves moved him emotionally or spiritually. "If I am a romantic," he later claimed, "my parents bear no responsibility for it."

An environment saturated with books and punctuated by secluded spaces known only to Warren and Jack encouraged the boys to exercise their imaginations. It is no great surprise that they did so together. Their home schooling, an arrangement settled upon by Albert and Flora that would not last long, limited the boys' exposure to other children, and thus they developed an unbreakable bond with one another. They became friends to a degree seldom enjoyed by brothers, sharing everything, including their fertile imaginations. All Warren and Jack needed was a venue where they could create the fantasy worlds both boys felt compelled to produce. They found it in a tiny attic space they called the Little End Room.

Located at the very top of Little Lea, this cramped space became their refuge. For one month between moving into Little Lea and Warren's departure for boarding school in England, the boys spent every free moment secreted away, high above their parents and the occasional servants hired by the family. In short order, the Little End Room became a world unto itself. In it, the Lewis brothers lived out different lives. They took paper and drew elaborate pictures of imaginary characters and laid out detailed maps of a land that existed solely in their own minds. They created stories about costumed animals who acted out very human dramas in a land Lewis called Boxen. Far from the prying eyes of their meddlesome father and beyond the reach of their demanding mother, the boys wandered across an imaginary landscape that synthesized all of the various influences acting upon them. Religious imagery, folktales, and myths came together to yield a rich, vivid collection of fantasies in the boys' "secret dark hole upstairs." This dark hole—or "study," as Lewis sometimes called it—became a forge within which the future author crafted the rough tools of creativity that he would hone only much later. Locked away with his brother, he thought and wrote with abandon.

Suddenly, in May 1905, the dream ended. Albert unceremoniously announced his plans to send Warren to school in England. He and Flora wanted a gentlemanly education for Warren, one that would soften his rough Irish edges and prepare him for a proper career. No school in Ireland could do that, so Warren had to leave. Lewis now lost his soul mate and best friend. Initially, he consoled himself by drawing nearer to his mother and by immersing himself in the day-to-day activities of his make-believe kingdom. Hidden in the Little End Room, Lewis wrote letters to Warren in which he recounted the mundane happenings in Boxen; he tried to write a play, kept a diary, and he read. By the age of ten, Lewis was not only trying his hand at short stories, but he was composing intricately detailed histories of Boxen and reading compulsively. Always precocious, he devoured literary classics such as Milton's *Paradise Lost* in record time.

Despite Lewis' frenetic creative pace, life at Little Lea moved slowly through the years. The peace was shattered in the summer of 1908, however, when doctors diagnosed cancer in Flora. By the end of August, her suffering worsened despite a desperate operation performed in her own bedroom. Albert grew sullen, and their young son worried incessantly as each began to ponder a future without Flora. Over the years, Albert and Flora had come to depend upon one another. Familiarity produced a bond that approximated love as closely as either person was capable of. Time had given the couple a peculiar connection based on respect and companionship—but now time had run out.

Jack was ill and in bed when his world changed. Throughout the house the sounds of men rushing back and forth could be heard. Lewis strained to make out the topic of countless hushed conversations in the hall outside his room. "It seemed to last for hours," he recalled, "then my father, in tears, came into my room and began to try to convey to my terrified mind things it never conceived before." Flora Lewis died at 6:30 in the morning on August 23, 1908. It was Albert's birthday.

Flora (shown here) and Albert Lewis had never truly loved each other throughout their marriage, but when Flora died, Albert Lewis could barely cope with the loss. In the wake of Flora's death, Albert began to grow distant from his sons, and soon sent both of them to school in England.

3

School Days

FLORA'S DEATH CAME as a crushing blow to Albert. For the first time in decades, he was alone. First he became bitter, and then resentful as the full force of his loss overwhelmed him. Albert's character began to change. His behavior became increasingly erratic and he slowly retreated into himself, shutting the boys out of his life. Lewis later recalled that not only had Albert lost a wife, but in his grief he was "really losing two sons" as well. At last, his father came to the conclusion that he could not raise Lewis alone. Albert sent him to join Warren at school in England.

The news of his impending exile from Little Lea devastated

Lewis at first, especially as it came so soon after Flora's death. In time he warmed to the idea, as getting away from Albert and the depressing pall that hung over the family home started to sound like a rather nice idea. If nothing else, moving to England would put Jack closer to Warren. Lewis left Ireland eagerly anticipating the upcoming reunion with his older brother, though he cherished the opportunity to study at Wynyard School far less.

Lewis arrived at Wynyard in September 1908, just in time for the new term. It was at this school that he learned to hate formal education. Whenever the adult Lewis reflected on the place, he referred to it as "a concentration camp." Perhaps this particular label was a bit of an exaggeration, but there can be no denying that Wynyard's headmaster, Robert Capron, was a brutal, sadistic man who tormented and abused the boys. Warren remembered how he had "seen him lift a boy of twelve or so from the floor by the back of the collar, and holding him at arm's length, as one might a dog . . . apply his cane to his calves." To make matters worse, the school itself offered little in the way of any genuine or meaningful curriculum. Almost nothing was taught, and even less learned. Lewis simply despised the place.

More disappointment was on its way. In 1909, Warren transferred to Malvern College some distance away. Although he himself would follow a year later, Lewis felt a deep sense of loss at the departure of his brother. He spent his days alone, trying get by the best he could. Jack took long walks with Wynyard's other boarders. Unsupervised exercise was one of the small consolations offered by the headmaster, who provided it more out of a lack of concern rather than any plan for the students' well-being. Lewis also spent untold hours reading. Books, especially the classics such as *Ben Hur* that he loved so much, helped him transcend the narrow confines of the school and enter into the familiar and comforting environs of fantasy. Still, he had to return to reality sometime, and when he did he only felt Warren's absence more keenly.

Worse than Capron's maltreatment was the fact that Wynyard required all of its students to attend church services twice each week, generally on the same day. For Lewis, this was the most hideous and excruciating torture he had to endure. Formal religion had always left him cold—Lewis felt that the scripted nature of the rituals his father had prized so highly emptied them of all meaning. Traditional services seemed dry and mind-numbing to a young boy with a hungry mind. He loathed his compulsory church appearances and felt somehow drained by them. The mere fact that one had to be forced to worship rather than being drawn to it voluntarily convinced Lewis that the religious assumptions he had grown up with were invalid and, therefore, useless. His ambivalence toward religion grew.

Yet Lewis' budding aversion to organized Christianity did not extend to the Bible. This, like so many other books, he read closely—not so much for spiritual solace but because its themes and images appealed to his love of fantasy. Great celestial battles, inner conflicts, love affairs, deceit, betrayal, demons, and angels—the Bible comprised them all. More importantly, it provided thematic scaffolds that lent its stories a strangely powerful literary force. Lewis was particularly fond of the darker motifs associated with evil and hell, especially when these came into direct conflict with good. The notion that good and evil contend with one another relentlessly for control over human lives stuck with Lewis. His interest in such contests increased and became more sophisticated over time. Many of his later works of fantasy and science fiction would be peppered with quasi-biblical scenes of sinfulness, conflict, and redemption.

Long walks and engaging books allowed Lewis to survive Wynyard long enough for good fortune to save him: the school officially closed in the summer of 1910. (Soon afterward, its headmaster Capron was declared insane.) Jack was free—free to return to Ireland and to some semblance of normality. For a brief time, he attended school near home. Then came thrilling news: Albert decided that Jack was to be sent off to study with Warren in England. Too young to be admitted to Malvern, Lewis would be enrolled at Cherbourg, a boarding school near Warren's campus. He would leave immediately in order to make it in time for the new term. The long night was over; Jack would be not only reunited his brother, but with his own creative self.

To say that he enjoyed Cherbourg would be to understate the case. The boy felt genuinely at peace there. First and foremost, he reestablished his cherished bond with Warren, though not without a few modifications dictated by the fact that both of the boys had grown up a bit. Since they were last together, Warren had become somewhat rambunctious. He spent far less time studying than he did carousing with his friends and smoking cigarettes, an offense for which the penalty was expulsion. At one point, he even tried to talk Albert into purchasing a motorcycle for him. Warren claimed that he merely needed a form of transportation. Albert knew better and refused. Warren then moved on to other more exciting pursuits, such as encouraging his little brother to be mischievous. One example of this was Warren's approval of Jack's latest obsession, smoking—a practice he began at the age of twelve and would continue until his death over fifty years later.

Cherbourg offered healthier pastimes as well. Lewis had access to books on a wide range of subjects. Still in love with the classics, he read them with renewed vigor. He also improved his writing through practice and produced essays on topics that spanned the spectrum from the composer Richard Wagner to school sports.

Perhaps the most significant event at the school, however, was Lewis' exposure to the views of Cherbourg's matron, Miss Cowie. Through close contact and mentoring, Cowie initiated him into the world of mysticism. What is known about this singular woman is limited, but it is clear that she held great sway over Lewis for the brief time they were together. Her beliefs seem to have been an odd amalgam of Eastern and Western interpretations of the divine presence. Miss Cowie appears to have advocated spirituality divorced from any organizational principle, let alone prescribed standards of worship. "Eclectic" best describes the set of beliefs Cowie passed on to Lewis; how much of it he absorbed is unclear. Her influence can be discerned only from the change that came over Lewis while at Cherbourg; he went into the school a lapsed Christian, but still Christian. He emerged claiming that the basis of formal church teaching and

Did you know...

While at Cherbourg School, Lewis tried his hand at sports, with limited success. He played on the school cricket team and worked hard to excel as both a batter and fielder. His efforts were not generally rewarded, however. The school newspaper reported that while Lewis was fair on offense, he could be considered "only very moderate in the field."

practice lay in "sheer illusion." He had become a confirmed agnostic with a propensity toward atheism.

Lewis' new ideas concerning God were accompanied by a fresh intellectual obsession—namely, a fascination with Norse mythology. His early exposure to this compelling literary form came through the vehicle of Richard Wagner's *Ring* operas. With their overtones of power and domination, Wagner's creations appealed to Lewis on a visceral level. They moved him by touching on some of his deepest emotions, especially his attraction to the dark imagery of evil and its inevitable conflict with good. He found himself drawn magnetically to Wagner and the Norse myths. Lewis later claimed that listening to Wagner and reading the Norse epics made him feel as if he were "returning at last from exile . . . to my native country." His interest went beyond merely fantasizing about gods of thunder or dead warriors feasting in the Norse heaven, Valhalla. Lewis utterly lost himself in the story Wagner turned into *Götterdämmerung,* or *The Twilight of the Gods*. While at home on vacation, he listened, enraptured, to Wagner's *Ride of the Valkyrie* for hours on end. Mysticism and the otherworldly power of mythology formed a potent mix in the young Lewis.

The powerful and concurrent influences of Miss Cowie and Richard Wagner exerted a pull on Lewis that accelerated his drift away from organized religion and eventually from Christianity itself. This slow movement had begun far earlier in Lewis' life, to be sure. It is doubtful that he ever really accepted his father's brand of faith, and he certainly would have rejected the pathological hatred evinced by Flora's father as he stood weeping in the pulpit at St. Marks. His affection for her notwithstanding, Lewis found Lizzie Endicott's anti-Catholic sentiments to be repugnant and surely below a woman of her character. Also, the awful experience of being subjected to alternating bouts of religious ritual and physical abuse at Wynyard and the consequent association of God with pain certainly must have persuaded Lewis that the answers he sought in life lay elsewhere. The unique fusion of mysticism and myth that took place at Cherbourg made Christianity seem bland, empty, and perhaps just a bit silly—no more so than when set in contrast to the romantic power of a spirituality free of God and given substance through the Norse epics.

At last in the fall of 1913, Lewis said goodbye to Cherbourg and entered Malvern College. There he pursued his new interests with a passion. Although he found the other students to be shallow and immature, he was willing to tolerate his classmates and teachers in exchange for long stretches alone in "The Grundy." This is what the college had nicknamed its library, the one place on campus where Lewis could retreat undisturbed into his own world. Hours upon hours were spent sitting, isolated and insulated from the reality outside, studying Norse literature and poetry. Lewis read everything he could find and anything that interested him in even a minor way. He developed an almost organic connection with The Grundy—"not only because it was a library," Lewis later wrote, "but because it was a sanctuary."

It was indeed a sanctuary, but one that could not offer protection forever. Indeed, as Lewis' private studies intensified, so did his college workload. Within a year, Lewis was working harder and longer than he ever had before. He became utterly exhausted and sank slowly into a deep depression. Lewis remembered being "tired, dog tired, cab-horse tired, almost like a child in a factory." Finally, he sent a letter to Albert begging to be withdrawn from Malvern and given an opportunity to rest. His father, having finally realized his dream of having both his boys away at an English

William Kirkpatrick, who would become Lewis' tutor and mentor, was instrumental in honing Lewis' mind into a finely tuned instrument. Not only did he instruct Lewis in five different languages, but also in the art of disputation, or verbal debate.

college, refused—and repeated pleas did nothing to move him. Only when Jack threatened suicide did Albert finally give in and remove his son from the college. He was soon placed in the care of Albert's former teacher, William Kirkpatrick. Kirkpatrick would serve as Jack's private tutor and mentor.

An imposing and blustery man, Kirkpatrick took charge of Lewis in a way the boy had never known. Under his tutelage, Lewis' academic skills improved dramatically. The boy mastered five languages ranging from Greek to German, honed his ability to analyze classic literature, and even gained a slightly better understanding of mathematics, although it remained his weakest subject. Perhaps most importantly, Lewis acquired the habit of disputation, or verbal debate, from Kirkpatrick. Certainly, untold evenings spent as a child listening to Albert and his guests debate politics over dinner had given Lewis a taste for argument, but in those scenes he had been a passive spectator. Kirkpatrick engaged him actively and most directly. Lewis had to be on his guard every moment of the day if he wanted to avoid being ambushed by his tutor. "You could not say something about the weather without being pounced upon," Lewis complained. "The most casual remark was taken as a summons to disputation."

Kirkpatrick's underlying goal in constantly challenging Lewis was far from idle torment, but to discipline his mind. His intellect, although formidable, was prone to recklessness. Lewis thought quickly but often without a clear focus or direction; his mind was strong but clumsy. Kirkpatrick's methods helped Lewis to rein in his intellectual powers and put them under his active control. He learned how to balance the rational requirements of serious study with an intense urge to let his mind wander into fantasy. Such maturity of mind would prove invaluable in the future.

Kirkpatrick, however, was also a convinced atheist. This Lewis absorbed as well. During the final of his two years with his tutor, Lewis came to reject organized Christianity in its totality. For at least five years, he had been drifting away from the religion of his childhood; now he openly broke from it. No longer was his disbelief a matter of disagreeing with ritual or dogma. Emboldened by his private studies and hardened intellectually by his exposure to Kirkpatrick's probing, Lewis proudly announced his liberation from Christianity. He swore that from that point on he would never go "back to the bondage of believing in any old superstition." To a friend, Lewis confessed that he had come to understand God to be "a spirit more cruel and barbarous than any man." C. S. Lewis had abandoned God—at least for the time being.

Lewis with his father Albert. In 1917, Lewis was admitted to Oxford University on a scholarship for performing well on the entrance exams—on all subjects except for math. During this time, World War I was raging, and students were enrolling in the Officer Training Corps and being sent to France to fight. Lewis would soon join them.

4

War and Peace

WILLIAM KIRKPATRICK COMPLETED his job by December 1916—well enough, it seems, for Lewis to be offered a scholarship to Oxford University. A scholarship, however, did not guarantee admission. Lewis still had to sit for and pass the Oxford entrance exams known as the Responsions, which he did in March 1917. As Kirkpatrick had predicted, Lewis performed superbly on all of the tests except mathematics—that portion eluded him, and despite his best efforts, Lewis could not pass it. He was admitted to the university, therefore, on a conditional basis contingent upon his retaking the math test and passing it the next go around.

Oxford in 1917 was a hectic place with freshmen settling in and upper classmen nervously waiting to find out if they were to be sent to France. War had been raging there for three long years, and the Oxford students all knew—and feared—the pattern already: admission to the university, enrollment in the Officer Training Corps (OTC), departure for France. Fate, though, was something Lewis had long since befriended. He took his OTC posting with a resigned shrug and tried to make the best of it. Lewis quickly made the acquaintance of another cadet from Ireland, Paddy Moore. Moore had been in the program for a while and already had received orders for the front. Lewis liked him and they became friends. Not long after, Paddy introduced his mother to Lewis. At the time, Lewis could not have known that he would develop a relationship with his friend's mother that would last until 1951.

Janie Moore came to Oxford to be with her son before he left for war. She most likely never intended to meet the man with whom she would share the rest of her life. Concerned as she was with Paddy's departure, she could not help but take notice of Jack and the affection she thought she glimpsed in his eyes. Neither she nor Lewis acknowledged what was obviously mutual attraction, nor did either of them immediately pursue it. Oxford during wartime was no place to explore one's emotions or begin relationships. Still, Lewis could not help but be drawn to Janie. Her Irish ways reminded him of home, and on top of being an avid reader, she was attractive and forceful. That Janie was separated but not divorced from her husband did not bother Lewis. Neither did the fact that, to the future dismay of many around Lewis, Janie was twenty-six years older than he. This age gap would be bridged eventually, but at the moment it presented an obstacle almost as formidable as the war.

Lewis received his orders for France in November 1917. Rather than rushing to be with his father as others might have done in similar circumstances, Lewis hastened to see Janie before he left. The bulk of the time between receiving his orders and shipping out was spent with her. Only when left with a mere forty-eight hours left in England did Lewis contact his father. He sent a somewhat cryptic telegram to Albert saying only "Report to Southampton Saturday. Can you come Bristol. If so meet at station. Reply Mrs. Moore's address." Albert replied that he did not understand what his son meant. By the time Jack received Albert's message it was too late. All

Did you know...

Lewis' father refused to visit his son at Oxford long before the incident just prior to embarkation. To be sure, there were practical considerations: the Irish Sea was infested with German submarines ready to sink any ship making the crossing to England, and Albert worried that his law practice would suffer. He also feared that his emotions might get away from him if the visit ended with a long goodbye. Yet Albert might not have wanted to see Lewis for a more personal reason; he had started drinking heavily and in all likelihood was something of an alcoholic by 1918.

he could write before leaving was a brief note telling his father, "Please don't worry."

Perhaps Albert really did not understand his son's telegram, as it was rather vague. Albert could not have known that Southampton was the port of embarkation for soldiers headed for France. Perhaps he was smarting at being passed over for Janie. Most likely he was simply fearful for Jack's life. When Lewis first entered OTC, Albert worried that "It is the beginning of a military career and the prospect covers me like a pall." Albert was convinced that his son would not "last as a ranker in the trenches." Whether out of confusion, anger, or fear on Albert's part, Lewis left for France without saying goodbye to his father.

Lewis arrived at the front on November 17, 1917, as a second lieutenant in the Somerset Light Infantry. He went almost immediately to the trenches. Considering the epidemic nature of illness in a place filled with cold, wet, hungry men, it is not surprising that Lewis fell ill within weeks of his stationing. He came down with a flu-like sickness known as pyrexia—or, as the soldiers called it, "trench fever." For the better part of a month, Lewis lay in bed recovering. He was in no hurry to return to his unit and enjoyed the respite the hospital offered, regardless of how poorly he felt. Yet recover he did, and back to the trenches he went.

For the next three months, February through April 1918, Lewis endured what he described understatedly as "a fairly rough time." The sights and sounds of war disturbed him greatly. The bloody, wounded men straggling along muddy roads, the mangled corpses, the shattered young minds staring out through blank eyes—all this unnerved Lewis and made him long for the warm, comforting distraction of a good library. Still, Lewis did his duty. He performed so well, in fact, that on one occasion he captured sixty Germans single-handedly. Typical of Lewis, he played the incident down, claiming that he actually had nothing to do with it. He protested that far from actively capturing the enemy soldiers, he simply was moving about the battlefield when he "discovered to my great relief that the crowd of field-grey figures who suddenly appeared out of nowhere all had their hands up."

Although he saw his share of fighting, Lewis argued that until "the great German attack came in the spring we had a pretty quiet time." Tedium, the weather, and army routine, he wrote, were his worst foes: "Through the winter, weariness and water were our chief enemies. I have gone to sleep marching and woken up again and found myself marching still." There was no downplaying the 1918 spring offensive, however. In one last push, the Germans threw their entire army and reserves at the British and French lines. Lewis now saw modern warfare in all its terrifying ferocity.

With bullets whining and shells booming, Lewis found himself on April 15 standing next to his unit's first sergeant when a misdirected English artillery round landed just yards away. The blast tore the young sergeant to pieces and knocked Lewis to the ground. Shaking himself out of the haze of concussion, Lewis dragged himself to an aid station. From there, he was sent to the hospital at Etaples. Lewis passed his time in bed quietly, eventually finding the strength to write Albert. Initially, the doctors had assured Lewis that his wounds were relatively minor, but their opinion later changed. He told his father that the puncture "under my arm is worse than a flesh wound, as the bit of metal which went in there is now in my chest." Still, Lewis, like his doctors, remained optimistic. He comforted Albert by saying, "I am told that I can carry it about there for the rest of my life without any evil results." That said, the good news was that he would be "sent across" back to England "in a few days, of course as a stretcher case." Second Lieutenant Lewis arrived in London in May 1918. For him the war was now over.

Lewis' London "hospital" was in reality a converted hotel, a fact that made his stay a bit easier to tolerate. Knowing that Janie intended to visit London to be near him allowed Lewis to rest even more comfortably. During his stay in the city, Lewis regained his strength to a point where he felt well enough to attempt to reinvigorate his relationship with Albert. Already his condition had improved sufficiently to allow him to travel short distances on day trips. One of his first stops was Great Bookham, the Kirkpatrick home, where he visited his old tutor. While visiting, he took the time to write Albert pleading with his father to come see him. In those letters, Lewis acknowledged that he had been a less than perfect son, but "please God," he promised Albert, "I shall do better. Come and see me. I am homesick, that is the long and the short of it." Albert, however, refused. He claimed to have bronchitis and to be unable to travel, although he still found the energy to maintain a busy work schedule. Lewis felt abandoned.

Still, his condition improved even if his relationship with his father did not. Soon Lewis was given the option of moving to a convalescent home. He chose one in Bristol so he could be close to Janie, who had a house there. As he settled in, he wrote Albert once more. This time he discovered that even humor could not move his father to visit him. Noting that it had been "four months now since I returned from France," Lewis remarked that "my friends laughingly suggest that 'my father in Ireland'

Janie Moore was the mother of a classmate of Lewis' at Oxford. Although she was twenty-six years older than Lewis, the two felt an instant attraction, and resumed their relationship after Lewis was discharged from his army hospital in London. Here Lewis is shown with Maureen and Janie Moore (far right).

of whom they hear is a mythical creation . . ." Albert still did not come, and now Lewis realized that father he wanted could not be conjured up out of nothing. It was too late to salvage a relationship with Albert; Lewis needed to get on with his life.

He had Janie, whose mere presence comforted him and gave him the closeness and feeling of security that Albert withheld. Warren remembered that his brother "was deeply hurt at a neglect which he considered inexcusable. Feeling himself to have been rebuffed by his father, he turned to Mrs. Moore for the affection which was apparently denied him at home." Lewis and Janie's fondness for each other grew. They even came up with nicknames for each other. She referred to Lewis as "Boysie," and he called her "Minto," an allusion to the candy mints Janie savored. His bond with Janie renewed Lewis' strength and stimulated creative energies that had been suppressed by the war and his long convalescence. He began writing again.

Although he had been assembling various of his poems since 1915, only after the war did Lewis bring them together into a single volume that he titled *Spirits in Bondage*. Lewis had always loved both reading and writing lyric poetry. Now he decided to try it out for public audience. Perhaps to insulate himself against failure, or perhaps in deference to an army command that frowned upon soldier-poets, Lewis chose to submit the work under the pseudonym "Clive Hamilton," his mother's maiden name. He took the time, for reasons unknown, to send a draft to Albert for comment. Seeming more distant than ever, Albert noted flatly that "for a first book—and of poetry—written by a boy not yet nineteen it is an achievement. Of course, we must not expect too much from it." In the end, *Spirits in Bondage* did moderately well after its publication, but, perhaps due to Albert's insensitive remarks, Lewis chose eventually to abandon poetry.

Lewis' lingering fears of being sent back to France evaporated permanently when news reached England of an armistice. Germany had collapsed, and due to his wounds, the army discharged him. Overjoyed, Lewis decided to make one final effort at building a bridge to his father. He packed a bag and left for Ireland, arriving unannounced just after Christmas, 1918. To his surprise, Lewis discovered that his brother had been granted leave and was already at Little Lea with Albert. They would spend the remainder of the holiday as a family. That

Christmas visit was one of precious few happy moments Lewis would spend in the presence of his father. Warren described the absolute elation he—and, to everyone's surprise, Albert—felt when Lewis turned up unexpectedly. Warren wrote in his diary that on December 27, he and Albert "were sitting in the study about eleven o'clock this morning when we saw a cab coming up the avenue. It was Jack! He has been demobilized, thank God. Needless to say there were great doings. He is looking pretty fit . . . In the evening there was bubbly for dinner in honour of the event: the first time I have ever had champagne at home." For a brief time, Lewis felt truly at home.

Lewis became a fellow at Magdalen College at Oxford University, a fact which pleased his estranged father greatly. Additionally, Lewis' fellowship added a steady source of income, with which he could better support himself, Janie and her daughter.

5

The Kilns and Christian Revival

DISCHARGED AND FREE, Lewis returned to Oxford in January 1919. His initial term there had been probationary, contingent upon his passing the math portion of the dreaded Responsions. Upon his return, he was surprised by the university's offer of full admission without requiring that he retake the test he had failed almost two years before. Like other returning veterans, Lewis fell under a new policy that exempted ex-soldiers from the testing component of the admissions process. If nothing else, his war service allowed him to settle in at England's preeminent university.

Later that year, fortune smiled once again. Janie Moore took up residence near Oxford in order to be closer to Lewis. The relationship between the young man and far older woman defied description. They had met through her son, but Paddy had been killed in France during the war; this should have severed the connection between his mother and Lewis, but it did not. In fact, they only grew closer. No one was quite sure what to make of all this. Warren, for one, disapproved of the relationship. "This Mrs. Moore business is certainly a mystery," he wrote to Albert. "It seems to me preposterous that there can be anything in it. But the whole thing irritates me by its freakishness." Whatever the rest of the world thought, Lewis felt a bond with Janie. He did not mind her age or the fact of her separation rather than divorce from her husband, nor was he dismayed by her occasional cruelty toward him. She filled a deep need within him, and that was all that mattered to Lewis.

The publication of *Spirits in Bondage* complemented the sense of fulfillment that came from being with Janie. This collection of poems represented Lewis' first effort to put on paper his conflicting beliefs about good and evil, God and Satan. Begun during his time with Kirkpatrick, *Spirits* was actually a compilation of reasons why God, if he exists at all, exists beyond the reach of human minds and souls. His impact is minimal, but worse yet is the fact that he simply does not care what happens to people. For Lewis to have his early musings on such weighty matters published, at the exact moment that he began to question any systematic belief in God, proved uniquely gratifying. The book's moderate success and his father's comments did nothing to lessen his satisfaction. Lewis was proud of his accomplishment, although it turned out to be his only serious work of poetry.

Published at last and in proximity to Janie, Lewis settled into a comfortable routine at Oxford. The summer of 1920 saw Janie and her daughter, Maureen, move into a house close to the university and paid for by Lewis. With Janie being so near and his career established, Lewis found it easy to settle into the kind of routine any academic would relish. He described this routine as his "usual life":

> I walk and ride out into the country, sometimes with the family, sometimes alone. I work; I wash up and water the peas and beans in our little garden; I try to write; I meet my friends and go to lectures. In other words I combine the life of an Oxford undergraduate with that of a country gentleman—a feat which I imagine is seldom performed.

Between the lectures, reading, writing, and Janie, Lewis could not have been happier.

Lewis also felt free to explore his growing doubts about God in public. He entered an essay contest in 1921 and submitted a paper on the topic of "Optimism." Lewis recalled the writing of the essay with great fondness, admitting that he "almost lived with my pen to paper." The time spent on the piece was "one of those rare periods . . . when everything becomes clear and we see the way before us." In the essay, Lewis stated flatly, with a rather matter-of-fact air, that he viewed God as a cold, distant entity who could not be bothered with mere mortals. "The trouble with God," he argued, "is that he is like a person who never acknowledges your letters so, in time, you come to the conclusion either that he does not exist or that you have got the address wrong." Lewis, by this time, came to believe that he had the address right, but no one lived at it.

Lewis completed his studies in August 1923 and received his bachelor's degree. Two years later, he became a fellow at Magdalen College, Oxford. Lewis telegrammed Albert saying simply, "Elected fellow Magadalen. Jack."

Albert recorded in his diary how he uncharacteristically "burst into tears of joy. I knelt down and thanked God with a full heart. My prayers had been heard and answered."

Lewis spent the intervening years between graduation and his fellowship quietly—studying, reading, and cultivating his relationship with Janie and her daughter. Money had always been tight, but occasional infusions of cash from Albert, who knew nothing of his son's financial support for Janie, helped float the "family" along. The Magdalen fellowship changed all that. Finally, Lewis had an income. The money enabled him to purchase a few luxuries for himself and Janie and to live with greater security and independence.

For the next five years, Lewis lived the life of a typical Oxford don. He taught, wrote, studied, and spent time with Janie. Yet his mind was anything but calm. His estrangement from Albert haunted him, as did his similar detachment from God. After debating with himself, Lewis began to play with the notion of reestablishing a connection with each. During the 1929 school term he even "knelt and

Did you know...

During his visit to the Whipsnade Zoo in September 1931, Lewis not only embraced God once again, but found out that he liked bears. Warren recalled how his brother thrilled at the sight of a brown bear that sat up and seemed to wave at Lewis. The writer decided at that moment that he simply had to have a bear as a pet. He never got one, but he did pick out a name for one just in case: "Bultitude." Lewis liked the name so much that he gave it to a character, "Mr. Bultitude," in his book *That Hideous Strength*.

prayed; perhaps the most dejected and reluctant convert in all England." Returning to God and religion was not easy, and Lewis had always been stubborn. His mind was too full to give the requisite attention to matters of the soul. When it came to God, his thinking had been murky. Albert's sudden illness cleared it for him.

In August 1929, Albert fell sick and underwent an emergency operation that determined the cause of his problems to be cancer. In the immediate aftermath of the surgery, Albert improved—no doubt due in part to an extended visit by Lewis, who stayed with him until he felt it safe to return to England. No sooner had he done so, however, than Albert's doctors summoned him back to Ireland. By the time he arrived, Albert had died. Lewis wrote to his brother explaining the whole matter:

> The operation . . . discovered cancer. They said he might live a few years. I remained at home, visiting him in the Nursing Home for ten days . . . By this time I had been at home since Aug. 11th, and my work for the next term was getting really desperate and, as [the doctor] said I might easily wait several weeks more and still be in the same position . . . I crossed to Oxford on Saturday, Sept. 22. On Tuesday 24 I got a wire saying he was worse, caught the train an hour later, and arrived to find that he had died on Tuesday afternoon.

And so the last remnant of Lewis' past drifted away.

The young Oxford don now settled into a period of intense reflection. Rather than feeling liberated by the passing of a man who never occupied a positive space in his life, Lewis experienced an overpowering sense of guilt. He conceded nothing to his father while the latter lived; meeting Albert halfway or trying to understand his point of view on things did not occur to Lewis. For this arrogance he felt guilty and

As their relationship deepened, Lewis and Janie went looking for a house to share together, and found one in 1930. They called it The Kilns, and invited Warren to come live with them. However, Lewis entertained friends and colleagues at Magdalen College.

ashamed. Lewis' spiritual awareness suddenly deepened, and he perceived the slight stirrings of religious sentiment in his heart. "It is not precisely Christianity," Lewis told a friend almost six months after Albert's death, "though it may turn out that way in the end."

Back in England, Lewis began to build a life freed from the shadow of his father. The twin focal points of his exertions now became Janie, and making sense of the spirituality starting to well up inside him. Lewis knew that his relationship with Janie had evolved past the point of merely keeping company. Whether or not he had fallen in love with her by this time is uncertain. Regardless of his emotional state, Lewis felt compelled to normalize what had been up to then a curious friendship. He proposed to Janie that they share a home together. Janie agreed and they began looking. Their search ended in July 1930, when they stumbled upon a small house they eventually dubbed The Kilns.

Warren, who came to visit shortly afterward, took one look at the house and "instantly caught the infection." He eagerly accepted his brother's invitation to move in with the couple and share The Kilns with them. The house's seller wanted £3,500 (about $8,000 in today's money). The sum was not an easy one for a university teacher to come up with—the money would have to be cobbled together. Lewis and his brother planned to sell Little Lea; that would bring in a large chunk of the purchase price, but not in time to pay for The Kilns outright. Janie dipped into a trust fund she had, Lewis pulled together all the cash he had available, and Warren came up with the deposit. Working together, they raised enough money to buy the house. The three moved in officially in October 1930.

Lewis, perhaps because he felt The Kilns ill-suited for entertaining or simply wanted to hold intellectual discussions in an intellectual setting, decided not to entertain his colleagues at the house he shared with Janie. His rooms at Magdalen College, which he maintained even after moving into The Kilns, served as a meeting place where Lewis and his friends could discuss their writing. On one of these occasions in September 1931, Lewis found himself in the company of the writer Hugo Dyson and J. R. R. Tolkien, the creator of the *Lord of the Rings* series. After dinner, the conversation turned to Lewis' views on God. He explained to his guests how he felt drawn to religion, especially Christianity, but "couldn't see how the life and death of Someone Else [Jesus Christ] 2,000 years ago could help us here and now." Lewis just could not comprehend the relevance of Christ in the modern world. Ever since Albert's death, he had wanted to carve out some place in his life for a divine presence, but could not overcome his aversion to what he saw as the empty superstition of organized religion.

Tolkien, who shared Lewis' obsession with mythology and fantasy, argued strongly that one did not have to link structure and belief organically as Lewis did. Tolkien claimed that it was possible to absorb and accept the core meaning of the religious story itself while jettisoning the associated doctrines, which in any case were a human imposition on the divine. One had to physically feel one's spirituality, Tolkien contended, much as the "elfin" characters in his *Ring* stories did. According to Tolkien, Lewis could have a relationship with God and faith in divine power without necessarily subscribing to any particular set of organized beliefs.

Hugo Dyson reiterated and elaborated upon Tolkien's points and kept up the pressure on Lewis. The three men talked until 3:00 A.M. before Tolkien finally went home. Giving Lewis no respite, Dyson picked up the theme of faith devoid of superstition. Taking the conversation outdoors, Lewis and Dyson walked the paths around Lewis' rooms for another hour discussing Christianity. Dyson held that Christianity brought a sense of calm and offered unique possibilities for personal growth to its believers. His argument resonated with Lewis, especially the part about positive change. Lewis had seen such change lately—his Oxford fellowship, finding the Kilns, his relationship with Janie—and this new Christian component seemed to provide a unifying framework for it all. After Dyson left, Lewis lost himself in thought.

Nine days after his conversations with Tolkien and Dyson, Lewis completed his personal Christian revival—his process of accepting once again the God he had rejected as a youth. He and Warren had chosen to go to the zoo one afternoon for an outing. Lewis recalled, in very ordinary terms, what happened that day: "When we set out I did not believe that Jesus Christ is the Son of God," he remembered, "when we reached the zoo I did." He quickly "passed from believing in

J. R. R. Tolkien, author of the Lord of the Rings *series, was one of the writers Lewis would entertain on a regular basis. One night in September 1930, Tolkien and the writer Hugh Dyson had a long conversation with Lewis on Christianity that would have a great effect on Lewis' own personal Christian revival.*

God to definitely believing in Christ." His journey back to God, like a modern-day prodigal son returning to his father, was complete. Perhaps Lewis could never return home to his real father, but to his heavenly one he could and did. On Christmas Day, 1931, C. S. Lewis went to church, took communion, knelt down, and declared his Christian revival over; it now became a Christian life.

Once Lewis had given himself over to a fully Christian life, he became more inspired than ever to write. His first book following his receiving communion was The Pilgrim's Regress. *He also started a group of fellow writers with Tolkien called the Inklings, who would gather regularly for discussion.*

6

Screwtape and Success

LEWIS GAVE EXPRESSION to his inner emotions by writing about them in allegory and metaphor. His pen clarified and explained Lewis' feelings not for his readers, but for himself. Writing acted as an outlet for his internal needs and desires that could not remain forever secreted away. This was never truer than in his sudden reversion to Christianity. No sooner had Lewis received communion in 1931 than he began working on *The Pilgrim's Regress*, a book that summarized and examined his return to faith. Published in 1933, *Regress* represented a virtual travelogue of a religious revival in which the main character, John (based on Lewis himself), wanders from the path of religion only to find his way home again. The story line loosely followed that of John Bunyan's *Pilgrim's Progress* in that a real, physical journey acted as a metaphor for the personal exploration of one man's journey of faith.

Lewis had come far on his road back to God; he had left much behind, and discarded far more. One part of the past that Lewis gladly relinquished was the home of which Albert had been so proud. He and Warren sold Little Lea and used the money to improve and develop The Kilns. The brothers purchased eight acres adjacent to the house and, with what was left over, had separate studies built for each of them. Lewis made sure that a little money was set aside for hiring a small staff of servants. Although the Lewises provided a sizable share of the funds for improvements to The Kilns, they made sure that Janie held the title to the house. Lewis himself was never good with money, and Warren's developing problem with alcohol prevented him from making any financial decisions. Most likely, giving Janie control over their shared home allowed Lewis to feel secure and convince himself that his bond with her had been strengthened.

As Lewis' fortunes improved, his circle of friends beyond Janie and Warren grew larger. He gathered around him a group of men who shared his literary passions. Unfortunately, Warren drifted in and out of this group according to his relative sobriety. Always fond of drinking, he now became a full-fledged alcoholic. Lewis worried about his brother constantly, but could do nothing to help him. Others around the author, however, applied their energies to more rewarding pursuits. They began meeting with Lewis on a regular basis to discuss literary matters and offer one another criticisms of and comments on their writing. Lewis eventually formalized their get-togethers by setting aside Thursday nights for a ritual of reading aloud and commentary. Working with Tolkien, he established the group of writers that came to be known as the Inklings.

For nearly fifteen years, the Inklings' weekly meetings served as a forum for the introduction of works in progress, playing out of ideas, and general stimulation of creativity. Although the group broke up rather unceremoniously in 1949 when no one but Lewis showed up for one of their gatherings, the regular encounters allowed Lewis and Tolkien an opportunity to develop exciting imaginative schemes and explore unfamiliar genres. This would prove crucial when it came to inventing the fantasy forms that could effectively communicate Christian ideals to a popular audience. By employing literary vehicles not commonly used for religious purposes, Lewis believed that faith might "be smuggled into people's minds . . . without their knowing it." He became a smuggler par excellence.

Lewis' first effort at delivering a Christian message via unorthodox means came with the publication of *Out of the Silent Planet* (1938). Few people expected him, as he correctly surmised, to camouflage morality the way he did. Lewis neatly packaged his essentially Christian tale as, of all things, science fiction, and did so with consummate skill. *Silent Planet* told the story of a young scholar's journey into outer space and subsequently to an alien world. The main character, Dr. Ransom, is kidnapped and taken to the planet Malacandra where he soon escapes. He is surprised to find that the planet's inhabitants are far from being the bloodthirsty monsters he presumed them to be. Indeed, the natives are a meek form of life that Ransom could easily dominate if he wished to do so. The splendor of Malacandra, as well as the timidity of its occupants, tempts Ransom to lord himself over the planet, but he valiantly resists.

Eventually he encounters an awesome creature, Oyarsa, who belongs to a larger group of similar entities responsible for governing the heavens. While in this being's presence, Ransom discovers that Earth is doomed to silence among the universe's worlds because its Oyarsa (a character Lewis describes in satanic terms) chose to seek power for himself alone. He failed and fell from grace, taking human beings with him. After this revelation, Ransom and his kidnappers are returned home to live with the knowledge of humanity's sentence never to be heard among the stars.

The Christian message of arrogance and ambition punished, trial and tribulation, and divine revelation comes across clearly in *Silent Planet*. Humans are condemned to suffer Lucifer's fate unless they can overcome the evil within themselves as Dr. Ransom did. Yet, more personally, the book is really Lewis' self-description of his own struggle to survive temptation and return home to God. Lewis had known his share of internal battles and had felt powerfully tempted by reason to abandon faith. Yet he now envisaged himself as transcending his sinfulness and coming into knowledge of the divine, much as his character did in *Silent Planet*. In any case, Lewis established a precedent with the book. Private turmoil and doubt were combined with public evangelization to create a new form of fiction that could only be described as Christian fantasy.

The pace of Lewis' writing now accelerated. He penned literary critiques and put together a series of essays focusing on personal reflection. Although he continued to write as broadly as ever, Lewis' newer pieces tended to concentrate on Christianity or Christian-inspired themes. He had a fresh purpose and direction to his writing that had eluded him in the past. The author's Christian beliefs lent coherence to his work, to be sure, but there was much more. His overwhelming desire to communicate what he saw as the core of Christ's message to a broad audience in terms they could readily understand gave his writing an intensity that no one missed. Faith brought self-assurance, and self-assurance put Lewis on the road to success.

The tempo of Lewis' career slowed temporarily in 1939 with the outbreak of World War II. Britain once again found itself at war with Germany, but this time the tiny kingdom stood alone against the might of the Nazi war machine. The conflict awoke Lewis' latent sense of duty and he volunteered for service. Brave though this offer was, the army had no room for a forty-two-year-old veteran with a piece of shrapnel in his chest. The recruiting office politely declined to induct the middle-aged author and suggested that he might consider signing up for the Home Guard, which Lewis promptly did. Warren was a different story. He had stayed in the army long after the armistice in 1918 and had only recently retired. Suddenly he found himself called up for service in France. Fortunately, his newly-revived military career proved short-lived. After being evacuated from Dunkirk in 1940, Warren was released from service. Both the Lewis boys would have to find other outlets for their energies during the war.

Warren continued his self-destructive struggle with the bottle. His brother, meanwhile, had been approached about giving a series of literary talks to Royal Air Force (R.A.F.) pilots as part of a morale-building program. He quickly accepted and was soon becoming quite popular among the young pilots to whom he spoke on any number of topics. It was a thankless job, but Lewis took to it with a missionary zeal. According to Tolkien, Lewis saw himself as some sort of modern-day saint spreading the Gospel: "The acceptance of the R.A.F. mission, with it hardship of travel to distant and nasty places and audiences of anything but the kind he was humanly fitted to deal with, lonely, cheerless, embarrassed journeys leaving little behind but doubt whether any seeds had fallen on good soil; all this way in its was an imitation of St. Paul." Lewis relished the comparison.

Not content with inspiring and enlightening the troops, Lewis made an even more personal contribution to the war effort. London and other major British cities had become very dangerous places since the beginning of the German bombing offensive in 1940, especially for children. The government decided that the safest refuge for young Britons lay outside the nation's urban centers. It instituted a program designed to evacuate children from the cities and called on average citizens to open their doors to these helpless war victims. Lewis heard his country's call and heeded it. He and Janie took in several children, or "evacuees" they were called. The experience left a lasting impression on Lewis. Not only did he realize that he actually liked young people, but he also recognized in them a potential audience for exactly the kind of Christian fantasy he had become so enamored of. He even perceived in his little guests the barest outlines of characters for future stories.

Lewis stayed active intellectually. His writing, in fact, began to mature in terms of its treatment of Christian themes. His mind became clearer and his work more bold. Clarity and boldness were the hallmarks of Lewis' first book on modern theology, *The Problem of Pain*, published in 1940. In this tightly constructed and lively work, Lewis experimented with bringing a rather arcane topic, "the intellectual problem raised by suffering," to a general public untrained in philosophical debate. *The Problem of Pain* represented a sincere effort to reach out to ordinary readers

During World War II, Lewis tried unsuccessfully to volunteer for service. He contributed in other ways, including giving morale-building literary talks to Royal Air Force pilots, and taking care of evacuee children, who actually inspired some of his youthful characters in future stories.

with a concept that might otherwise be inaccessible. The challenge was to offer up intellectual fare in common language. Few writers had ever truly succeeded in this, but Lewis was determined. As he put it, "Any fool can write *learned* language. The vernacular is the real test. If you can't turn your faith into it, then you either don't understand it, or don't believe it." A new expressive force was coalescing within Lewis—a vital blend of Christian morality, mythical fantasy, and popular fiction. Writing in plain English, Lewis hoped to draw people closer to God without their ever consciously knowing it.

Successful though *Silent Planet* was, Lewis' second work of fiction far surpassed it. Writing with astounding vitality and using the full thrust of his imagination, Lewis pounded out a book that soon brought him incredible fame. Finished in February 1941, he titled the work *The Screwtape Letters*. Set up as a series of correspondences between a pair of devils, a veteran deceiver named Screwtape and a novice named Wormwood, the letters trace out their joint program for ensuring the damnation of one young man who frustrates his fiendish pursuers by becoming a Christian. Lewis designed the story so that his readers could discern themselves and others in the descriptions of humanity given by Screwtape to Wormwood. If people saw themselves the way a devil would, Lewis figured, they could also conceive of themselves as Christians modeled after the main character. While lacing his story with hilarious bits of observational humor, Lewis never lost his focus on the very serious issue of how one goes about avoiding temptation and gaining salvation.

Screwtape reached Lewis' audience initially through a series of installments in the Anglican weekly *The Guardian* beginning in May 1941. The public received the work well and Lewis earned a substantial amount of money, which he promptly donated to charity. Pulled together into a single volume, *Screwtape* was published as a book in 1942, amplifying the total effect of the story line beyond anything Lewis had dreamed of. As a book, *The Screwtape Letters* was wildly successful. People read it with abandon, forcing the publisher to reprint the book eight times in the first year. Perhaps more importantly, the work's publication generated an avalanche of letters that soon buried Lewis in paper. He received so many letters, in fact, that he asked Warren to come work for him as a secretary. Together they answered readers' questions, responded to their comments, and worked to keep up the momentum. As sales climbed, money poured in, all of it channeled into a charitable account, the Agape Fund, set up and managed by the brothers. Lewis wanted the proceeds from *Screwtape*, a book about devils, to serve a Christian purpose.

The book's popularity can be explained by the fact that it was so easily digested by average readers. Its language was plain and unpretentious, and its chosen medium — personal letters — was completely familiar to almost everyone. Feeling that they were reading someone else's private correspondence gave people a sense of intimate knowledge — a closeness that comes from knowing the plan of events as they unfold. Even more engaging was Lewis' strategy of exploring temptation from a devil's point of view. Here he capitalized on human nature; people always seem to comprehend evil more readily than good. Lewis' habit of pointing out common foibles bordering on sinfulness, furthermore, convinced his readers that they were surveying a very real human landscape in the pages he wrote.

Sales figures for *The Screwtape Letters* attested to the fact that Lewis had won over the reading public, but this was the middle of the twentieth century. Books now had to compete with radio for people's attention. Millions of nonreaders sat passively in front of their radio sets unaffected by the written word. In order to reach them, Lewis would have to swallow hard and take to the airwaves. Lewis never liked radio, and later despised television, but he was enough of a realist to understand that radio would put him in touch with people who might not otherwise be exposed to the Christian message in his books.

Thus, in the summer of 1941, when the British Broadcasting Company (BBC) contacted Lewis and asked him to give a series of on-air talks on religious topics, he accepted. His radio career began in August with fifteen-minute lectures delivered every Wednesday night. His fame grew almost uncontrollably. Warren struggled to keep up with the incoming mail. The BBC begged Lewis to give more talks. People everywhere debated Lewis' ideas, argued about his views, and professed to either love or hate him. Yet no one

Did you know...

Lewis was not only convinced of the physical reality of God, but believed Satan was real as well. "The proper question," he once said, "is whether I believe in devils. I do. That is to say, I believe in angels and I believe that some of them . . . have become enemies to God . . . These we may call devils." Lewis concluded that at the head of this evil host stood "Satan, the leader or dictator of devils."

could ignore his potent message of Christian redemption. A friend, commenting on Lewis' broad popularity at the time, recalled how he had been in a smoky English pub one night when a Lewis broadcast began. As the author started to speak, a burly, rough-edged soldier turned to his comrades and said, "You listen to this bloke . . . He's really worth listening to." Lewis became so well known after the radio talks that his colleagues at Oxford grew envious of his success and snubbed him at faculty functions.

Lewis' pen wrote even more furiously as his fame grew. In rapid succession, he published a series of books: *Beyond Personality* (1942); two sequels to *The Silent Planet*, *Perelandra* and *That Hideous Strength*, both in 1943; *The Abolition of Man*, also in 1943; and a follow-up to *Screwtape*, *The Great Divorce* (1945). Finally, in 1952, Lewis published a collection of his BBC broadcasts under the title *Mere Christianity*. As his books rolled off the presses, the author felt not simply satisfaction but an over-powering confidence.

Suddenly Lewis had the professional capital, the raw capability to touch millions of lives through the sheer power of his books and the sound of his voice. The years after *Screwtape* saw the disparate elements of Lewis' imagination gel into a vibrant mix of mythology and moral absolutes. Lewis found that he had the unique ability to harmonize religion, fantasy, and reason in the pursuit of solutions to the great moral and ethical riddles of modern life. He could now transform his inner, private conversations into very public explorations of good and evil, what it meant to have faith, and what it meant to call oneself a Christian.

A map of Narnia, the fantasy world that Lewis created with his book **The Lion, The Witch and the Wardrobe**. *Its success would eclipse that of* **The Screwtape Letters** *as children around the world took to the series with great zeal, and was arguably one of Lewis' greatest works of fiction to "smuggle" themes of Christianity and spirituality.*

7

Narnia

WHILE LEWIS' CAREER was reaching its height, his relationship with Janie was crumbling. Beginning with the purchase of The Kilns, they drifted apart. Lewis spent more and more time on the Oxford campus and less with Janie. His friends were not hers, and her interests became increasingly meaningless to him. By 1950, Janie had become demanding and argumentative. She seemed to be ill all of the time, and she used her maladies as an excuse to lash out at everyone around her, including Lewis. Alternately sullen and agitated, Janie took perverse pleasure in assigning Lewis pointless menial tasks such as walking her dog—an animal he abhorred. Warren, never fond of "Mrs. Moore," disliked her intensely by this time.

Lewis was hard at work on a new book, *Surprised by Joy*, published in 1955, and so he paid as little attention as possible to Janie's souring. He responded to her bitterness by simply putting more distance between them, using his writing as a refuge. In April 1950, Janie fell out of bed and was hospitalized. Lewis tried to miss her, yet he confided to a friend that his life was "both more physically comfortable and psychologically harmonious" without her around, although he continued to visit her daily. During her stay, she contracted influenza and died on January 12, 1951. Warren "mourned" her passing by getting so drunk that he missed Janie's funeral. He asked rhetorically in his diary, "I wonder how much of his time she did waste?" Lewis for his part never gave in to regret. He defended his commitment to her by saying only that "I have definitely chosen and I don't regret the choice."

Conflicted though his emotions might have been, Lewis certainly felt a degree of relief at Janie's passing. She had indeed become a burden, but Lewis never forgot how Janie had filled in for his father, and his mother, at a time when he desperately needed companionship and compassion. Still, her death liberated Lewis to complete the transformation that began with his Christian revival and found expression in books such as *Silent Planet* and *Screwtape*. Lewis began to write as never before. He discovered creative talents as yet unknown, even to himself, and longed to exploit them. The final product of all this was Lewis' signature work, the climax of years of personal and professional evolution, was the Narnia Chronicles.

"I am not quite sure," Lewis once remarked, "what made me, in a particular year of my life, feel that not only a fairy tale, but a fairy tale addressed to children, was exactly what I must write—or burst." The urge to craft a fantasy, a Christian fantasy for children, overwhelmed Lewis as Janie languished in her hospital bed. Writing at breakneck speed, Lewis produced a series of books that told the story of an awesome contest between good and evil in a faraway land known as Narnia. While putting the collection together, he wrote an average of one book a year. One volume in particular, *The Voyage of the "Dawn Treader,"* took only two months to put on paper. Each book in the series represented the sum of Lewis' most elaborate imaginings and the culmination of a lifetime's worth of introspection and self-reflection. Yet for all their complexity, each book began modestly. "All my seven Narnian books," Lewis noted, "began with seeing a picture in my head." Those pictures, filtered through religion and myth, emerged from Lewis' pen as modern-day parables.

No book in the Chronicles demonstrates this better than the first and most widely read of them all—*The Lion, the*

Did you know...

Lewis told Warren of the arrival of his evacuee guests by commenting on how sweet and honest they seemed. He found them to be refreshing. "Our schoolgirls have arrived," he wrote, "and all seem to me . . . to be very nice and unaffected creatures and all most flatteringly delighted with their new surroundings." He studied the girls so closely that some Lewis scholars attribute his well-developed girl characters in the Narnia Chronicles to the experience.

Witch, and the Wardrobe, published in 1950 just before Janie's death. In one slim volume, Lewis brought to bear an imagination freed, once and for all, from every constraint. The book owed its immediate background and setting to his wartime care for the young evacuees he and Janie took in, but its inspiration came from Lewis' desire to offer the Christian message to as many readers of all ages as possible. Lewis did indeed intend for *The Lion, the Witch, and the Wardrobe* to have an audience beyond children. He firmly believed that "a children's story which is enjoyed only by children is a bad children's story."

The book follows four evacuated children as they travel through the portal of a magic wardrobe and emerge into the land of Narnia. There, a battle is raging between forces loyal to the good lion king, Aslan, and the disciples of the fiendish White Witch. One of the children falls under the witch's spell, compelling his friends to fight for his redemption. The children are subsequently caught up in the drama of Aslan's quest to save Narnia from the clutches of evil. Through betrayal, Aslan is eventually killed, but he rises again to lead one last offensive against the powers of darkness. In this titanic struggle, he destroys the White Witch and brings a new day to Narnia.

Although the similarities are obvious, Lewis did not attempt merely to repackage the story of humanity's salvation through the death and resurrection of Christ for a younger audience. Rather, he redesigned it as it would have unfolded in an alien reality. As Lewis put it, "Suppose there was a world like Narnia and it needed rescuing and the Son of God . . . went to redeem it, as He came to redeem ours, what might it, in that world, all have been like?" *The Lion, the Witch, and the Wardrobe*, in other words, was more than a reconfiguration of the Christian story; it comprised a totally fresh application of Christian ideals. The overall effect was to make those ideals, and the Christian model, seem universal.

Lewis followed his first Narnia tale with six others: *Prince Caspian* (1951), *The Voyage of the "Dawn Treader"* (1952), *The Silver Chair* (1953), *The Horse and His Boy* (1954), *The Magician's Nephew* (1955), and *The Last Battle* (1956). All of the books allowed Lewis to insert God into fantasy and myth, reconciling two seemingly polar opposites. Nearly every influence that had acted upon Lewis at one time found expression in the Chronicles. All the notions and beliefs, understandings and questions swirling around in the author's head came out on the pages of the Narnia books. They represented the inner world of a man striving to bring himself closer to God through the process of sharing his Christianity with others.

Lewis wanted more than anything else to tell the story of Christ's struggle to save people from evil—the evil within each one of them—and bring peace to their lives. He accomplished that not just by writing, but by writing in simple words through an engaging, readily grasped medium. The Narnia fantasies conveyed what was to Lewis the reality of God's design.

The Chronicles were well received by its primary audience, children, and swiftly rose to the level of classic literature. Lewis' contemporaries, however, were for the most part less impressed. J. R. R. Tolkien positively hated the books, criticizing them severely. Tolkien protested that the books mismatched various mythological themes, stirring them together into a messy fictional soup. He claimed, furthermore, that a close reading revealed sloppy writing and careless construction.

Some of Tolkien's harshness might have emerged out

Lewis' friend Tolkien was actually critical of the Narnia stories, taking issue with the mythologies utilized as well as the writing. However, Tolkien may have been reacting out of jealousy, as his own Lord of the Rings *had met with a cool reception by the Inklings — and he had written* Lord of the Rings *in seven years, while Lewis wrote the seven Narnia books in six years.*

of his resentment of the speed at which Lewis wrote the Chronicles. Tolkien took seven years to write the *Lord of the Rings*—and here Lewis had written seven books in six years! Envy probably caused him to read Lewis more critically than he otherwise would have. Tolkien's own writing—in particular, his drafts of *Lord of the Rings*—had also been snubbed by the Inklings while they were together, and lingering resentment over his treatment must have clouded his thinking. The Inklings had been so blunt and even sarcastic in their critiques of Tolkien's work that he eventually refused to read any of it at the group's meetings. Lewis, being the driving force behind the circle of authors, bore the brunt of Tolkien's anger from then on.

Tolkien aside, most critics felt that while the Narnia books were well written, they lacked imagination and were unduly complex. None of them figured that the series would gain the status it did, but children knew better. In both Britain and the United States, young readers devoured Lewis' tales. The Puffin paperback series still lists Lewis as one of its most popular authors. The stories he wrote, because no one else would "write the books I want," have been bestsellers for almost 50 years. Lewis could not have predicted such fame and success, nor could he have anticipated the love that would shortly enter his life.

American Joy Gresham came into Lewis' life first as a fan of his writing, then as an aggressive suitor. Lewis, a bit shaken by Joy's forthrightness, constantly made sure to have chaperones whenever meeting her for meals. However, he found her to be quite charming, and invited Joy to spend Christmas with him and his family.

8

Surprised
by Love

WITH THE PUBLICATION of the Narnia Chronicles, Lewis'
creative life was complete. Emotionally, however, he felt a deep
void. He had welcomed God back into his heart, but a peculiar
empty space remained. Lewis had thought that faith would
translate into fulfillment, and to an extent it did. Divine compassion sustained Lewis' soul, but without the simple love of
another person Lewis had no way of realizing God's love on a
daily basis. Compassion, devotion, companionship, and the
exhilaration of touching the hand of someone who really cared
remained abstract concepts to Lewis. He could understand

love intellectually, but he was denied the experience of it physically. The abrupt arrival of Joy Davidman Gresham in London changed all that.

Joy Gresham materialized just as Lewis was in the midst of writing his autobiography, the coincidentally titled *Surprised by Joy*. The word joy had always been a metaphor for the soothing presence of the divine in Lewis' life; now it took concrete form in a woman by the same name. The changes she brought and the depth of Lewis' feelings for her did indeed surprise him. Lewis had never given much thought to love, and as a consequence had never really known it. His relationship with Janie had been serious and complex, but few around Lewis would have described it as love.

Joy was something different altogether; in many ways, she stood in stark contrast to Lewis. An American Jew, she immersed herself in politics from a young age in a manner Lewis would have abhorred. She became a loyal Communist who embraced ideology to the same degree that he shunned it. Joy spoke her mind in contrast to the generally reserved Lewis, and took chances where he opted for the security of routine. Still, in two crucial respects, her life mirrored his. For one, Joy began writing as a girl. While studying at Hunter College in 1934, she won a short story prize. A friend recalled how "Joy seldom dated. When she did go out, her escorts were older men seriously interested in literature."

By the time she had turned 25 years old, Joy had published a novel and tried her hand at professional writing. Yet perhaps more importantly, the once-atheist Joy had returned to God. As a young woman she, like most Communists, had rejected any notion of a supreme being. Adversity, however, changed her outlook. After experiencing the true depth of disappointment that this world can bring,

Joy refocused her attention on the next. Thus two writers with a profound appreciation for the power of faith had found each other at just the right moment.

Joy Davidman married William Gresham in 1942 after he had already endured one failed marriage. If Joy had not figured it out before, the reason for the earlier disaster became painfully apparent. Gresham was an ugly man—physically and emotionally. His face, to begin with, had been disfigured by severe acne. He suffered from tuberculosis which left him pale and weak. Unable to handle the common disappointments and misfortunes of life, Gresham had attempted suicide once. Now he had descended into alcoholism. Drunk, depressed, and often abusive, he at one point nearly abandoned Joy altogether.

As their relationship began to disintegrate, Joy and her husband jettisoned Marxism and replaced it with another all-encompassing worldview: Christianity. "All my defenses . . . went down momentarily," Joy wrote of her conversion, "and God came in." Both Joy and William claimed to have returned to God, but only she took the reunion seriously. For her, Christianity became a refuge, a new emotional scaffold that brought some semblance of order and normality to her life. Yet what Joy gained from faith, above all else, was a profound experience of contentment. She gave her soul to God, in much the same way she would later give her heart to Lewis.

Joy met Lewis initially through his religious writings. Having read his work carefully, Joy corresponded with him briefly and soon became determined to meet him in person. Lewis' writing had inspired her earlier conversion, and now she sought his advice as her marriage collapsed. First, she needed to get to England. Leaving William and their two sons in the care of her cousin, Joy traveled to Britain in

September 1952. Not long after she arrived, Joy boldly invited Lewis and his brother to lunch. Warren declined and Lewis would have backed out of the engagement entirely had it not been for a friend who offered to act as a chaperone at the last minute. She thus introduced herself to Lewis and both of them detected an almost simultaneous attraction. Joy had an agile mind and a quick wit, and she could more than handle herself in an intellectual debate. Lewis found all of these traits thoroughly enchanting.

Joy's assertive personality, however, and her obvious intention of taking any relationship with Lewis beyond mere acquaintance frightened the somewhat introverted author. Her overtures unsettled and confused him. Lewis tried avoiding her for a while, but Joy persisted. Lunches followed one after another, notwithstanding the fact that Lewis refused to dine with her alone. Finally, Lewis gave in and invited Joy to visit him for Christmas at The Kilns. That holiday was the most memorable for Lewis since the time when he, Warren, and Albert had been together in 1918.

Did you know...

Joy was notorious for her brash and even abrasive behavior. She spoke her mind plainly, and rarely took into account the setting or the sensibilities of the other people present. While at an Oxford faculty lunch, for instance, Joy inquired as to the location of the women's restroom by blurting out, "Is there anywhere in this monastic establishment where a lady can relieve herself?"

Most of Lewis' associates found Joy to be abrasive, crude, and prone to swearing. Lewis laughed at those same qualities; in fact, he tended to laugh at whatever came out of Joy's mouth.

For two weeks, Joy stayed at The Kilns, cooking dinner for Lewis and his brother, laughing and drinking with them as if she had been born into their family. Joy was there, doing her best to impress Lewis and win over Warren, when she received a letter from her husband asking for a divorce. Gresham claimed to have fallen in love with Joy's cousin, into whose care and arms he had consciously been delivered by Joy herself. She had to have known that, with things as bad as they were in the marriage, and with Gresham's reputation as a womanizer, her husband and cousin would almost certainly be drawn to one another. Joy wanted to give him an excuse to leave as much as she hoped he would go. Gresham told her in his letter that it would be best for them to split up and for her to get "married to some real swell guy."

That is exactly what she had planned to do all along. Seizing the opportunity to end a disastrous and destructive marriage, Joy returned to America and granted her husband a divorce. Her only condition was that she be allowed to take their sons back to England with her. He acceded to her one demand and their union dissolved. Joy could now insert herself into Lewis' life with a clear conscience.

Joy established a permanent residence in London after returning and continued seeing Lewis. Lewis, meanwhile, made the wrenching decision to leave his beloved Oxford for a choice position at Cambridge University. After a warm welcome from the faculty and students, Lewis settled in and immediately fell victim to a crippling bout of writer's block. The man for whom words had always come so easily simply could not find any. Despite his best efforts, he just could not write. His pen languished unused on blank paper while its master searched in vain for the mental pictures that gave substance to his stories.

Joy came to the rescue. Sensing Lewis' growing panic at not being able to write, she made it a habit to visit and sit with him while the two "kicked a few ideas around until one came to life." Lewis took her advice even though Joy claimed that she could not "write one-tenth as well as" Lewis. Joy was unable to plant ideas in the head of an author who wrote what he "saw," but she could and did "tell him how to write more like himself." In the end, Joy proudly reported that the man she idolized "finds my advice indispensable."

By August 1955, Joy and her sons had moved into an apartment paid for by Lewis. Through the fall and winter, the bond between Lewis and the woman he accepted as his best friend deepened. He was never one to throw his emotions around carelessly; in fact, Lewis feared the prospect of opening himself to scrutiny by another, even if that person loved him. For that reason, Lewis kept himself just out of Joy's reach. He comforted himself by claiming that such a state of affairs was perfectly natural, especially for a very private man. The game of love, as Lewis put it, required that "while the one eludes must the other pursue."

The game abruptly ended in early 1956. The British government refused to renew the permit that allowed Joy to remain in England. If she did not gain status as a British national, she would be forced to leave the country. Lewis proposed a solution—civil marriage. He assured his skeptical brother that the "marriage was a pure formality designed to give Joy the right to go on living in England." Warren remembered how Lewis had even given his word that Joy would not move into The Kilns. To do so would signal her status as a "real" wife. Yet there was far more

In 1955, Lewis paid for an apartment in England for Joy and her two sons (shown here) to move into. Soon, the two were faced with a dilemma when the British government refused to renew the permit that allowed her to stay as a visitor—so Lewis decided that a civil marriage would be the solution that would allow Joy to stay in England.

involved than practicality or convenience. Joy's son, Douglas, recalled later how deeply his mother and Lewis cared for each other. "There were never two people alive in the history of the world," he said, "more in love than Jack and Joy." The two were married on April 23, 1956.

Tragically, soon after their marriage, Joy became very ill and was diagnosed with bone cancer. However, Lewis was determined not to let her illness get in the way of their blossoming love, including procuring a religious wedding and taking Joy to Greece.

9

Living and Dying with Joy

LEWIS' DISCOVERY OF happiness in his relationship with Joy gave him a genuine sense of completeness in his life. All the empty spots in his heart that even God left vacant seemed to be filled by Joy. A climax of sorts had been reached in Lewis' lifelong struggle to find spiritual and emotional fulfillment. Sadly, the tranquility that settled on the author lasted a mere two months—in June 1956, Joy became seriously ill. That October, Joy suffered a minor fall. She had noticed a gradual weakening in her legs and pain that seemed to reach up into her chest. Paying little attention to it, Joy went on, never mentioning anything to Lewis. The pain grew worse, though, and sometimes she could barely walk. The fall brought it all home. She was taken to the hospital where she received a diagnosis of bone cancer.

Joy's illness only drew Lewis closer to her. "Never have I loved her more than since she was struck down," he told a friend. Lewis, in fact, became determined to live out as much of his newfound love for Joy as time would permit. He wanted to experience all those things he had missed. Chief among these was the utter contentment and warm security that comes from loving and being loved. Lewis did not know how long they had left together—"a reasonable probability of some years . . . a real danger that she may die in a few months"—but he refused to be cheated. Disease, and even the knowledge of certain death, would not stop him from absorbing as much love as he could in whatever time remained.

Both he and Joy wanted desperately to make their union legitimate in the eyes of God. A civil ceremony gave them social privileges and state sanction, but only a religious one offered the hope of a marriage that might transcend death itself. Eternity came only through the intercession of heaven; no license or government certificate could do that. Also, Joy demanded the right to die somewhere other than a cold hospital ward. The Kilns was where she wanted to be when the end came. So, Lewis lobbied the Church of England for a religious wedding that would consecrate his relationship with Joy. Based on her divorce, however, the Bishop of Oxford refused Lewis' repeated petitions. The panicked writer cast about for some alternative and found it in a close friend who was both a minister and sympathetic to Lewis' cause.

The clergyman agreed to perform the service, and on March 21, 1957, he joined the Lewises in the presence of Jesus Christ. The ceremony took place at Joy's bedside as she was too sick to do otherwise. Warren described how they "all gathered in Joy's room," and how he watched his brother suffer. Both men knew she would not survive. All that kept Lewis going, according to Warren, was the promise of "dying under the same roof" as Joy. Warren just hoped that when it arrived, there would "be no pain at the end."

Joy improved dramatically after the wedding, but now Lewis fell ill. His doctors told him it was acute osteoporosis, and that there was little they could do for him. Already in severe pain, Lewis could barely move as his bones lost precious calcium. Still, he comforted himself by imagining that somehow Joy might recover. Occasionally, she gave him reason for such hope by improving slightly, but overall her condition only got worse. For two long years, the couple endured their afflictions together. At last, both felt well enough to take a brief trip to Ireland. They enjoyed the visit immensely, and Joy seemed actually to be doing better.

Soon after their return home, though, the cancer flared up, this time worse than ever. The doctors held out hope for some sort of turnaround and encouraged Lewis keep his spirits up, yet he knew better. He did not feel justified in asking God to do more than He had already done in bringing him and Joy together in the first place. He wrote that "we've enjoyed the fruits of a miracle. I am not sure it would be right to ask for another." Although Joy had long since lost any such hope, she still retained her sense of humor. She once commented dryly that she had "so many cancers at work on me that I expect them to start organizing a union." Lewis laughed with her but feared that time was running out. Before it grew too late, he wanted to take Joy to Greece, a place she had always longed to visit. It was their first real vacation together, and it would be their last.

Joy had a splendid time in Greece. They toured the country at length, visiting the ruins at Mycenae and taking part in an Easter service at a Greek Orthodox cathedral. They explored the Greek countryside and ate out every night, laughing the night away. The pair even visited the temple at Delphi and prayed to the god Apollo for a cure. None came, but Lewis was thrilled nonetheless to see Joy so happy. Upon their return to England, however, her condition worsened markedly. She was soon hospitalized and underwent surgery to remove a large tumor. The operating surgeon was not hopeful; Joy asked to leave the hospital and Lewis obliged. They returned to The Kilns to await the inevitable in the warm confines of the only place either one ever truly thought of as home.

Early on the morning of July 13, 1960, Lewis "was awakened by [Joy] screaming." He ran to her and, finding her in excruciating pain, called for the doctor. When he arrived, one look was enough to tell him that Joy's condition was deteriorating rapidly. The doctor "gave her a heavy shot" and rushed her to the hospital in an ambulance. There Warren recalled Joy being conscious "and in very little pain, thanks to the drugs." She rested for the remainder of the day, drifting in and out of her drug-induced haze, "and died peacefully about 10:15 the same night." Her dying words were for her husband's ears. "I am at peace with God," she told Lewis. "You have made me happy."

Once more alone in the world, Lewis tried to lose

Following Joy's death, Lewis was also discovered to be ill by his doctor. He would have to undergo blood transfusions, but it was for naught. When he was diagnosed with kidney failure and suffered a heart attack, Lewis knew that his time was near, and looked forward to the end.

himself in his work. Not knowing any other way to deal with his pain, Lewis wrote, pouring out his sorrow in a book he entitled *A Grief Observed*. In its pages, Lewis explored his feelings of loss and loneliness in the only way he could; he dissected his grief in an effort to understand what it all meant. Joy had been everything to him, he wrote, she had been his friend, his wife, "my trusty comrade." Next to writing, Lewis found no better place to rest his tired heart than in prayer. Grief propelled him into an even deeper comprehension of his faith and his God. He missed Joy, but told himself that their separation could be nothing but temporary if the heaven they both believed in truly existed.

Above all, his prayers helped him to move beyond mourning his loss to a celebration of the time they had together and a hope for reunion. Lewis remembered how Joy had promised to meet him on the day he died. "If you can—if it is allowed—come to me when I too am on my death bed," he asked. "Allowed!" Joy replied. "Heaven would have a job to hold me; and as for Hell, I'd break it into bits." Lewis would wait for that day, but not long. He could feel the last chapter of his life approaching.

Almost a year passed before Lewis began to feel sick. His doctor prescribed a strict diet and ample rest. He also recommended that Lewis give up the cigarettes, but after about fifty years of smoking it proved difficult—so he decided not to follow his doctor's orders, at least as far as tobacco went. Lewis argued that if he gave up smoking he "should be unbearably bad-tempered. What an infliction on my friends." Lewis stated defiantly, "Better to die cheerfully with the aid of a little tobacco, than to live disagreeably and remorseful without." What time he had to live would be enjoyed.

Smoking or not, Lewis rested, ate well, and read. The one imposition he detested was the need for blood transfusions. His doctors knew that part of his problem was that his kidneys were not functioning as they should, so they recommended periodic transfusions. Lewis' wit, however, remained as strong as ever, even if some of his internal organs did not. Once, after a rather painful transfusion session, he remarked that he felt "some sympathy for Dracula. He must have led a miserable life."

By the spring of 1962, Lewis had improved to the point where he finished one book and began thinking of another. An inexplicable weakness stopped him, though. Every day, it seemed, he required longer and longer periods of rest. He tried to work but could not get up enough energy. A visit to the doctor ended with a diagnosis of kidney failure; the damage that had been done was permanent and irreversible. He was admitted to the hospital and there suffered a severe heart attack. The staff felt so certain he would die that they called a priest to come and give him his last rites. Fearing that Lewis had only minutes to live, the priest set to work immediately. After having been anointed with oil, to the surprise of everyone present, Lewis suddenly woke up and began talking. God, it appeared, was not quite ready to receive his soul.

Did you know...

Lewis' death, on November 22, 1963, was overshadowed by an American tragedy. On the same day that Lewis died, President John F. Kennedy was assassinated in Dallas, Texas. Coincidentally, British writer Aldous Huxley, the author of *Brave New World*, died the exact same day. Neither writer's passing captured the headlines as did the shooting of Kennedy. Nevertheless, the world lost three great men at one time.

Back at The Kilns, an invalid Lewis settled into the forlorn routine of a man devoid of purpose. Day blurred into day, one uneventful hour stretching into the next. His schedule was a dreary exercise in boredom—bland lunches, fitful naps, tea, smoking, then finally to bed to await another colorless morning. Lewis could have worked harder at recovery but understood the futility of trying to prolong his life; he welcomed the release death would bring. He confided to Warren that "I have done all I wanted to do, and I'm ready to go." To a friend, Lewis wrote cheerfully, "Don't think I am not happy." He claimed to be enjoying himself immensely; he was even reading the *Iliad* again, and according to Lewis, getting more from it than he had as a youth. Lewis remarked to another correspondent that he was "not sure that old age isn't the best part of life. But, of course, like autumn it doesn't last."

Just one week shy of his 64th birthday, Lewis looked forward to a typical day at home. In the morning, Warren checked in on him, only to be told, "I'm all right." The day proceeded as usual with Lewis taking to his favorite chair after lunch, where he promptly fell asleep. Warren, concerned that his brother might be uncomfortable, moved him into bed. Suddenly, at 5:30 in the evening, Warren heard a crash in Lewis' room. Running in, he found his brother on the floor, breathing but unconscious. Frantically, Warren tried to revive him, but after a few brief minutes, it was over. Clive Staples Lewis died quietly on November 22, 1963. On that fall evening, the great author entered what his main character in *The Last Battle*, the lion Aslan, called "the Shadowlands": a world where his "term is over: the holidays have begun. The dream is ended . . . the end of all the stories."

Yet for Lewis, as Aslan said, it was only "Chapter One of the Great Story which no one on earth has read; which goes on forever, in which every chapter is better than the one before."

C. S. Lewis' writing legacy transcends that of mere "children's author," and it is evident that he explored many themes throughout his writing, including religion and philosophy.

10

A Life Remembered

IT IS TEMPTING to view C. S. Lewis primarily as a children's author. Most people have had little exposure to his writing beyond the Narnia Chronicles. The average reader probably has not explored much beyond the occasional grade-school book report on *The Lion, the Witch, and the Wardrobe*. It is easy, therefore, to conceive of Lewis as a writer limited to spinning stories of fantasy worlds where the fears and hopes of childhood are played out. Yet calling Lewis a "children's writer" implies that he consciously wrote for young people as a discrete category of readers, and that this particular audience served as a focal point for his creative talents.

In this assumption, one could not be more wrong. Lewis did not choose fantasy any more than he chose other genres. He wrote what he had to in order to communicate the Christian message that became so dear to him—there was nothing self-conscious in it. Lewis did not feel that fantasy was a patently juvenile form of fiction. Imaginary schemes had been a part of his life since his own childhood and continued to be so as he matured. Certainly the stories he told in the Narnia Chronicles held a special appeal for younger readers, but that was more a function of a society that denied adults the necessary freedom to wonder than anything else. Christian fantasy of the type Lewis wrote was never meant to be constrained by the classification "children's books."

It would be unfair as well to hang the label of religious writer on Lewis. No one doubts that his faith was indisputably genuine. Lewis perceived God as a physical presence and a profound influence. He himself said that "the story of Christ is simply a true myth: a myth working on us in the same way as others, but with this tremendous difference that *it really happened*." More so than most people, he understood his spirituality in almost visceral terms. Religion shot through his entire being—Lewis thought of God, he felt God, and he understood God emotionally and intellectually. As Lewis arrived at the conclusion that he finally grasped the divine in all its complexity, he sought to share that knowledge. He set to the task of bringing God, through the Christian principles of sacrifice and salvation, to the masses of people who Lewis believed wallowed in ignorance.

Still, his religion and his writing were subjective aspects of the author. Lewis never wrote about religion as if it were some objective entity that stood outside of human experience. Lewis wove God into the fabric of perception and sensation. He looked inside for the divine and wanted others to do likewise. Perhaps more importantly, Lewis wanted people to rely on their ability to imagine God. He felt this to be a natural outgrowth of the innate human capacity for feeling over thought. Lewis, in fact, contended that "the imaginative man in me is older, more continuously operative, and in that sense more basic than . . . the religious writer."

Nor would it be fitting to describe Lewis as a philosopher. It is true that questions concerning the nature and understanding of existence consumed him. Throughout his career, Lewis tried to reconcile the conflict between reason and emotion. He labored tirelessly, and in the final analysis successfully, to bridge the wide chasm that too often separates intellect and imagination. Lewis considered it artificial to distinguish between what one knows and what one imagines. Rather than differentiate between reality and fiction, Lewis argued that they needed to be seen as part of a larger whole, one complementing the other. Thinking, and considering how people conceive of the world around them and their place in it, came naturally to Lewis. He did not choose to think deeply or write about the results of that process—it just happened. Lewis, to be sure, had a philosophy that he honed and adjusted as the years passed, and there can be no doubt that many of his works can only be categorized as philosophical examinations. Still, Lewis' thinking had a practical goal. While questions suffice for most of those we call philosophers, Lewis wanted answers, and he desired above all else to apply those answers to everyday life.

Lewis wrote children's books, explored religious questions, and considered the purpose of existence neither to entertain nor even to educate in the strict sense of the word. God, Narnia, and the essence of grief were stages in Lewis' long process of life that he felt compelled to share with others. His writing, more simply put, was designed as an invitation to his audience to tag along with him as he embarked on a journey of self-discovery. The destination was only the last part of getting there; the *journey* was the point. Books were the expressive vehicles that transported a thoughtful person from one place to another in his and their minds. Lewis once said that everyone moved inexorably toward either salvation or damnation, and that "All day long we are, in some degree, helping each other to one or other of these destinations." This cooperative effort drove Lewis, rewarded his exertions, and, in the end, fulfilled him.

Did you know...

Lewis' death devastated Warren, upsetting him so much that he could not attend his brother's funeral on November 26, 1963. Rather than be at the service, Warren climbed into bed and promptly got drunk. When he sobered up, Warren arranged for the placement of a gravestone on which was written a fitting epitaph: "Men must endure going hence."

Lewis wanted people to join him as he mused over the connection between the mind and the heart. When, if at all, did they meet? How did they interact? Questions such as these absorbed and occasionally confounded Lewis. He tried to propose answers based on a combination of personal reflection, learned study, and outright fantasizing—all done in the presence of others, his readers. Out of this amalgam, Lewis crafted a new lens through which the world could view itself. By accompanying him on his journey, Lewis' readers were encouraged to consider more deeply their own final destination.

Lewis' life was neither closed or private. He welcomed visitors warmly and treated his readers as companions. They enjoyed with him exciting visits to fantastic worlds— from Boxen to Malacandra to Narnia. Lewis' audience rediscovered the comforting presence of God and the reassurance of salvation through Jesus Christ with him. Readers also suffered with Lewis the terrible disappointment of love lost and the grief of having someone torn away long before they should have been. Lewis believed that in order for one to "see things as the poet sees them, the reader must share his consciousness and not attend to it." He did not want people to *read* him; Lewis left people no option but to *be* with him.

Lewis' books were really just friendly discussions between traveling companions. Rather than being finished products, they were more like scratch paper on which the author worked out ideas. He really was not making any final statements, but rather setting up future exploration, examinations, and analyses. Lewis always had just one more thing to write, one more question to grapple with, one more picture to draw from the seemingly inexhaustible

Deborah Winger and Anthony Hopkins portrayed Joy Gresham and C. S. Lewis in the 1993 movie Shadowlands, *which depicted their unique relationship. Both Lewis' life and his work continue to capture readers' imaginations well beyond his death.*

store in his head. Perhaps it is fitting, then, to think of C. S. Lewis as something akin to a work in progress in the end. Much like his writing, he was never quite complete. His life was always being revised and freshly drafted, a story in search of a fitting conclusion.

1898 **November 29** C. S. Lewis is born in Belfast, Northern Ireland.

1905 **April 21** The Lewises move in to their new house called Little Lea.

1908 **August 23** Flora Lewis dies at home on Albert's birthday.

September 18 Albert sends Lewis to Wynyard School.

1911 **January** Lewis transfers to Cherbourg School.

1913 **September 18** Lewis enters Malvern College.

1914 **September 19** Lewis' education under William Kirkpatrick begins.

1917 **March 20** Lewis sits for the Oxford exams and passes all of them except for mathematics.

June 8 Lewis is introduced to Janie Moore and their relationship begins.

1918 **April 15** Metal splinters from a stray British shell wounds Lewis near Arras in France.

1919 **January 13** Lewis returns to complete his studies at Oxford.

March 20 Lewis' first book, *Spirits in Bondage*, is published.

1925 **May 20** Magdalen College elects Lewis a fellow.

1929 **September 25** Albert Lewis dies in Ireland.

1930 **October 10–11** Lewis and Janie Moore move into The Kilns.

1931 **September 28** Lewis embraces Christianity once again on a trip to the zoo.

1933 **May 25** Lewis' book on his return to faith, *Pilgrim's Regress*, is published.

1942 **February 9** *The Screwtape Letters* is published.

1950 **October 16** The first of the Narnian books, *The Lion, the Witch, and the Wardrobe*, is published.

1951 **January 12** Janie Moore dies.

1952 **September 24** Lewis meets Joy Davidman Gresham.

1956 **April 23** Lewis and Joy are married after she divorces her husband in America.

1956 **October 19** Joy is diagnosed with cancer.

1957 **March 21** Lewis gets his wish of a religious marriage ceremony. The service is performed in Joy's hospital room.

1958 **July** The Lewises go to Ireland. After their return, Joy's cancer worsens.

1960 **April 3–14** Lewis takes Joy to Greece for one last vacation together.

July 13 Joy Lewis dies of cancer.

1961 **September 29** Lewis' thoughts on Joy's death are published as *A Grief Observed*.

1963 **June 15** Lewis is admitted to a nursing home. His health deteriorates rapidly.

November 22 C. S. Lewis dies.

By far, C. S. Lewis' most popular books are *The Lion, the Witch, and the Wardrobe* and *The Screwtape Letters*. Both books describe confrontations between good and evil, and each reflects Lewis' desire to bring the Christian message to people in terms they could readily comprehend.

THE LION, THE WITCH, AND THE WARDROBE

In *The Lion, the Witch, and the Wardrobe*, four young children, evacuees from wartime London, step through a magic wardrobe that serves as a portal into the fantasy kingdom of Narnia. There the children discover a land troubled by the diabolical White Witch. After one of their number falls prey to the Witch's powers and joins her, the other children offer their assistance to the majestic lion-king, Aslan, who has sworn to defeat the witch and bring a new day to Narnia. In concert with Aslan, the children draw the witch into a climactic battle that ends with her overthrow and the salvation of their friend.

THE SCREWTAPE LETTERS

The Screwtape Letters tells a similar tale, but from a rather unique perspective. Here the main character is a crafty old devil by the name of Screwtape who plots the temptation and damnation of an unsuspecting young man. Working through his inexperienced nephew and apprentice devil, Wormwood, Screwtape endeavors to deceive his victim into abandoning righteousness for the dark allure of hell. The focus of Screwtape's project and of Wormwood's prodigious if somewhat clumsy efforts eludes capture by deepening his faith, even in the face of repeated setbacks and personal tragedy. Screwtape and Wormwood are ultimately frustrated when their intended target, who has avoided every trap set for him by the devilish pair, is killed in an air raid without having forsaken his soul. Final victory, as in *The Lion, the Witch, and the Wardrobe*, belongs to the powers of heaven.

Spirits in Bondage: A Cycle of Lyrics (1919)

The Pilgrim's Regress: An Allegorical Apology for Christianity, Reason, and Romanticism (1933)

Out of the Silent Planet (1938)

The Problem of Pain (1940)

The Screwtape Letters (1942)

The Abolition of Man: Reflections on Education with Special Reference to the Teaching of English in the Upper Forms of Schools (1943)

Perelandra (1943)

Beyond Personality: The Christian Idea of God (1944)

That Hideous Strength: A Modern Fairy Tale for Grown Ups (1945)

The Great Divorce: A Dream (1946)

The Lion, the Witch, and the Wardrobe (1950) [Narnia Chronicles]

Prince Caspian: The Return to Narnia (1951) [Narnia Chronicles]

Mere Christianity (1952)

The Voyage of the "Dawn Treader" (1952) [Narnia Chronicles]

The Silver Chair (1953) [Narnia Chronicles]

The Horse and His Boy (1954) [Narnia Chronicles]

The Magician's Nephew (1955) [Narnia Chronicles]

Surprised by Joy: The Shape of My Early Life (1955)

The Last Battle (1956) [Narnia Chronicles]

Till We Have Faces: A Myth Retold (1956)

A Grief Observed (1961)

C. S. Lewis brought dozens of fascinating characters to life that people of all ages know well and remember fondly. Among these, Aslan and Screwtape stand out. Of course, anyone who has read *The Screwtape Letters* recalls easily the unforgettable character of Wormwood. Children still recognize much of themselves in Peter, Edmund, Susan, and Lucy, the boys and girls who ventured forth through the wardrobe into Narnia. Science fiction fans would find it difficult to erase from their imaginations the intrepid Dr. Edwin Ransom, the hero of *Out of the Silent Planet*. Still, Aslan and Screwtape are uniquely memorable by virtue of their roles as archetypes.

ASLAN, Narnia's majestic lion-king, possess qualities that carry mythical associations—courage, dignity, and righteousness in authority. Lewis went so far in *The Lion, the Witch, and the Wardrobe* as to cast, albeit unintentionally, a Christ-like aura around his fantasy monarch. Aslan never wavered in his defense of good. He did not shrink from conflict with evil, and he stood ready to sacrifice his own life for his subjects' salvation. Rewarded with resurrection, following his murder by the White Witch, Aslan used the gift of life to bring the powers of darkness to their knees. In a final allusion to the Christian story of sacrifice and redemption, Aslan, after crushing the White Witch's armies, triumphantly inaugurates a new day for Narnia.

SCREWTAPE stands as the antithesis of Aslan. He is an indefatigable purveyor of sin and destruction. Resentful of humanity's nearness to the heart of God, Screwtape sets himself to the task of sowing discord and rancor throughout God's creation, laying waste to earth's beauty one mortal soul at a time. Confident to the point of hubris, Screwtape is self-congratulatory and supremely arrogant. Yet under it all, the counsel offered by Screwtape to Wormwood belies an acceptance of the power and majesty of God. Indeed, Screwtape's searing hatred of humanity is born of fear and a grudging recognition of hell's subordination to heaven. Screwtape is at once cunning, loathsome, pathetic—and ultimately destined to fail.

It is perhaps the unending struggle between quintessential good and raw evil embodied in their characters that makes Aslan and Screwtape C. S. Lewis' best-known characters. Lewis put them each at the center of a struggle central to the very construction of what it means to be human. Certainly, if nothing else, these two characters represent the fundamental, lifelong tension that Lewis personally experienced and sought to comprehend within himself and explain to others.

Duriez, Colin. *The C. S. Lewis Encyclopedia: A Complete Guide to His Life, Thought, and Writings*. Wheaton, Illinois: Crossway Books, 2000.

Green, Roger Lancelyn and Walter Hooper. *C. S. Lewis: A Biography*. New York: Harcourt, Inc.,1974.

Sayer George. *Jack: A Life of C. S. Lewis*. Wheaton, Illinois: Crossway Books, 1988.

Schultz, Jeffrey D. and John G. West, eds. *The C. S. Lewis Readers' Encyclopedia*. Grand Rapids, Michigan: Zondervan Publishing House, 1998.

Wilson, A. N. *C. S. Lewis: A Biography*. New York: W.W. Norton and Company, 1990.

Adey, Lionel. *C. S. Lewis: Writer, Dreamer, Mentor*. Grand Rapids, Michigan: Eerdmans, 1998.

Carpenter, Humphrey. *The Inklings: C. S. Lewis, J. R. R. Tolkien, Charles Williams and Their Friends*. Boston: Houghton Mifflin, 1979.

Dorsett, Lyle. *Joy and C. S. Lewis*. London: HarperCollins, 1994.

Duriez, Colin. *The C. S. Lewis Handbook*. Grand Rapids, Michigan: Baker Book House, 1992.

Filmer, Kath. *The Fiction of C. S. Lewis: Mask and Mirror*. New York: Macmillan, 1993.

Ford, Paul. *Companion to Narnia*. San Francisco: Harper Row, 1980.

Harris, Richard. *C. S. Lewis: The Man and His God*. London: Collins Fount, 1987.

Karkainen, Paul A. *Narnia Explored*. Old Tappen, New Jersey: Revell, 1979.

Kilby, Clyde S. and Douglas Gilbert. *C. S. Lewis: Images of His World*. Grand Rapids, Michigan: Eerdmans, 1973.

Myers, Doris. *C. S. Lewis in Context*. Kent, Ohio: Kent State University Press, 1994.

Sammons, Martha C. *A Guide Through Narnia*. London: Hodder, 1979.

Schofield, Stephen, ed. *In Search of C. S. Lewis*. Los Angeles: Bridge Publications, 1984

http://www.cslewis.org
[The C. S. Lewis Foundation]

http://personal.bgsu.edu/~edwards/lewis.html
[C. S. Lewis and the Inklings]

http://www.discovery.org/lewis/cslewis.html
[Lewis Legacy]

http://www.comnett.net/~rex/cslewis.htm
[C. S. Lewis Quote Page]

http://cslewis.drzeus.net/
[Into the Wardrobe]

page:

10: Used by permission of The Marion E. Wade Center, Wheaton College, Wheaton, IL

17: Used by permission of The Marion E. Wade Center, Wheaton College, Wheaton, IL

20: Used by permission of The Marion E. Wade Center, Wheaton College, Wheaton, IL

27: Used by permission of The Marion E. Wade Center, Wheaton College, Wheaton, IL

30: Used by permission of The Marion E. Wade Center, Wheaton College, Wheaton, IL

38: Used by permission of The Marion E. Wade Center, Wheaton College, Wheaton, IL

40: Used by permission of The Marion E. Wade Center, Wheaton College, Wheaton, IL

47: Used by permission of The Marion E. Wade Center, Wheaton College, Wheaton, IL

50: © Hulton Archive/Getty Images

56: Used by permission of The Marion E. Wade Center, Wheaton College, Wheaton, IL

59: © Bettmann/CORBIS

60: Used by permission of The Marion E. Wade Center, Wheaton College, Wheaton, IL

67: © Hulton Archive/Getty Images

72: THE MAP OF NARNIA by Pauline Baynes © C.S. Lewis Pte. Ltd. Reprinted by permission.

78: © Hulton Archive/Getty Images

80: © Michael Peto Collection, University of Dundee Archive Services

87: Used by permission of The Marion E. Wade Center, Wheaton College, Wheaton, IL

88: Used by permission of The Marion E. Wade Center, Wheaton College, Wheaton, IL

95: Used by permission of The Marion E. Wade Center, Wheaton College, Wheaton, IL

98: © Bettmann/CORBIS

104: © Howard Jacqueline/ CORBIS SYGMA

Cover: © Burt Glinn/Magnum Photos

Frontis: © Michael Peto Collection, University of Dundee Archive Services

JOHN DAVENPORT holds a Ph.D. from the University of Connecticut and currently teaches at Corte Madera School in Portola Valley, California. He lives in San Carlos, California, with his wife, Jennifer, and his two sons, William and Andrew.